A Hill to Die On

A Hill to Die On

Will Stickle

CONTENTS

The Enduring Legacy of Think and Grow Rich

There are few books that outgrow their time and step into something mythic. Think and Grow Rich is one of them. It's not just a book—it's a manifesto, a mirror, a magnet. Published in 1937 during the Great Depression, Hill's work didn't land with a whisper. It landed with a thud, like a gold bar dropped on the desks of the desperate. It promised wealth, yes—but more than that, it offered agency in an age of collapse. It dared people to believe that their thoughts were weapons. That their minds were currencies. That they weren't slaves to their circumstances, but sovereigns over them.

And that's why it still matters.

Hill never gave the masses a road map. He gave them a mirror and a match. Look in it, and if you don't like what you see, burn it all down and start again. That was the real power of Think and Grow Rich. Not in the 13 principles he supposedly distilled from the likes of Carnegie, Ford, Edison, and other titans. But in the quiet, radical whisper between the lines: you are the cause of your life—no one else.

That idea alone makes the book dangerous. That's why the system tolerates it but never teaches it. Schools churn out employees and followers. Hill wrote for leaders and outlaws. For the man who looks around at the chaos, the debt, the mediocrity, and says, not me. For the woman who refuses to settle for scraps when she knows she was born for sovereignty.

Hill didn't invent ambition. But he spiritualized it. He didn't just tell you to work hard—he told you that thought, when fused with desire and belief, could become physical reality. This was metaphysical capitalism. Prosperity gospel without the preacher. You didn't need church. You didn't need school. You needed a burning desire and a refusal to quit.

And millions took it to heart.

The book went on to sell more than 100 million copies. That's not just influence—that's infrastructure. Think and Grow Rich became a blueprint for everyone from broke hustlers to billion-dollar CEOs. Bob Proctor built a career on it. Tony Robbins quoted it before he had a stage to stand on. Grant Cardone, Daymond John, Steve Harvey—if you follow the threads, many roads lead back to Hill. And not because he had all the answers. But because he gave people permission to ask the right questions.

What do I really want?

Why don't I have it yet?

What am I willing to become to get it?

These are not passive questions. They demand action. And action is something the modern world despises. It prefers distraction. It wants you doped up on comfort, numbed by Netflix, broken by bureaucracy, and pacified by promises. Hill's book—then and now—is a middle finger to all of that. It doesn't offer safety. It offers sovereignty.

Of course, critics hate that. They'll remind you Hill was never rich himself. That he was sued, accused of fraud, and always on the brink of financial ruin. And they're right. He didn't live the clean, tidy success story he sold. But here's the uncomfortable truth—neither do most revolutionaries. Hill was part philosopher, part snake-oil salesman, part preacher, and part outlaw. The legacy of Think and Grow Rich is wrapped in contradiction because the man who wrote it was wrapped in contradiction.

And yet, the message holds.

In a world begging for handouts, Hill dared to say, demand more of yourself. In a culture that blames, whines, and wallows, Hill whispered, get to work. He didn't teach you to beat the system. He taught you to build something so strong within yourself that the system became irrelevant.

And that's why the book won't die.

Because every generation needs to hear it again. Because every time a man wakes up broke, lost, or humiliated by the smallness of his life, there's a chance he'll reach for that battered old book and hear the voice that says: you can change everything—if you're willing to change yourself.

That voice doesn't age. That fire doesn't burn out. Not when the world is full of people hungry for more but too afraid to admit it. Not when mediocrity is sold as virtue and failure is blamed on systems instead of self.

Hill gave us a weapon. He didn't care if we liked him. He wanted us to win. And whether he lied about Carnegie or not, whether he failed at half his ventures or all of them, he still managed to light a fire under the feet of the willing.

And for that reason alone, Think and Grow Rich remains a hill worth dying on.

Napoleon Hill's Influence on Modern Self-Help

Napoleon Hill didn't just write a book—he launched a movement. A cultural virus. A framework of thought that metastasized into everything from TED Talks to TikTok influencers, from boardroom seminars to bedroom vision boards. If you're reading a book, watching a guru, or listening to a coach who says things like "believe it and you'll see it," you're hearing Hill—whether they know it or not.

Before Hill, "success" was mostly reserved for the aristocrats and industrialists—the ones with inherited land, money, or bloodlines. After Hill, success was democratized. At least in theory. Suddenly, the janitor had the same weapon as the CEO: mindset. The playing field wasn't level, but Hill handed you a ladder and told you to climb it anyway. No excuses. No waiting for permission. Just desire, decision, and discipline.

He planted that seed in the middle of the Great Depression, and it grew into a global industry. Today, that industry is a multi-billion-dollar monster that Hill never lived to see. Every seminar, coaching program, podcast, and best-selling business book owes him royalties in spirit. He gave them the template. He gave them the language.

Desire. Faith. Auto-suggestion. Persistence. The Master Mind.

These weren't just ideas—they became doctrine. And they got watered down, repackaged, rebranded, and sold back to us in every flavor imaginable. Tony Robbins took Hill's fire and turned it into a stadium rock concert. Bob Proctor took the Law of Attraction and wrapped it in a whiteboard and a suit. Rhonda Byrne simplified it into a glitter-covered gift bag called The Secret, selling the illusion that wishing and journaling could replace work and grit.

But they all followed the trail Hill blazed.

Even the tech world, drunk on disruption and "10X" growth, is standing on Hill's shoulders. The startup culture worships at the altar of mindset. Vision, belief, boldness—they're just new words for Hill's original formula. Hell, even Silicon Valley's obsession with "manifestation" is little more than autosuggestion in a Patagonia jacket.

But here's the irony: Hill's message was radical, but it was also raw. It wasn't soft. It wasn't gentle. He didn't tell you to "just be yourself." He told you to become something more. To forge yourself through hellfire if necessary. He didn't coddle. He challenged. He said, If you're not getting what you want, it's your fault. And in a world now terrified of blame, that's considered offensive.

And yet, the modern self-help scene picks Hill's bones clean while sanitizing his soul.

They'll preach positivity but leave out pain. They'll chant affirmations but skip the part about sacrifice. They'll talk about goals but not about obsession. Hill's original work was a blueprint for psychological warfare—you vs. you—but most modern gurus don't have the stomach for that fight. So they sell dopamine instead. They slap Hill's face on a motivational quote and never mention the demons he battled.

Because here's the truth no one wants to say: Hill was not a well-adjusted man. He wasn't a perfect example. He was broke more often than not. He battled depression. He bent the truth when it suited him. But that's what makes his influence real. Because most of the people buying self-help books aren't polished. They're desperate. Hurting. Drowning in mediocrity. Hill didn't float above them—he was one of them. He wrote from the hole, not the throne. That's why he connected.

Modern business culture leans heavily on his work, too—whether it admits it or not. Every sales training with a script, every corporate mindset module, every performance coaching program has Hill's fingerprints all over it. Ask a thousand successful entrepreneurs what book changed their life, and Think and Grow Rich will make the top five every time. Why? Because it doesn't teach tactics—it teaches identity. It doesn't care what you do—it cares who you are when you do it.

That's the core that keeps echoing. Hill's influence lives in the tension between accountability and possibility. Between blunt responsibility and blind belief. That paradox is what gives the modern motivational world its teeth—when it dares to bite. Most don't. They peddle comfort. Hill sold confrontation.

He built a bridge between mysticism and pragmatism. Between metaphysics and capitalism. He didn't just tell people how to succeed—he dared to tell them they already had everything they needed inside, and they'd have to drag it out with blood and fire. That message terrified institutions. It still does.

Because if people really believed what Hill was saying? If they truly embraced the idea that their mind is the first cause of their reality? Politicians would have less power. Banks would have fewer slaves. Therapists would lose patients. Governments would lose excuses. The cult of victimhood would collapse overnight.

But most won't go that far. They'll settle for 10-minute morning routines and Instagram quotes. They'll eat the frosting and leave the cake. That's the dark side of Hill's legacy—he laid the groundwork for greatness, and the world built a shopping mall on top of it.

Still, the blueprint is there.

And for those who aren't afraid of it—for those willing to own their lives instead of lease them—Hill's influence is still a nuclear weapon. It can still shatter the concrete of mediocrity. Still break the cycle of dependence. Still ignite something ancient and violent and true inside the individual.

That's why his legacy matters. Not because he was perfect—but because his message is pure fire when you read it right.

3

A Word on Why This Is "Unofficial"

This is not a Foundation-approved fairy tale. This is not a polished documentary with backing from the estate. This is not a celebration. It's not a smear campaign either. This is the book Hill probably wouldn't have wanted written—but it's the one that has to be.

Why?

Because Napoleon Hill became more than a man. He became a brand. A doctrine. A monetized legacy. And once that happens, truth becomes a liability. The Napoleon Hill Foundation has turned his name into an industry. Clean edges, tidy narratives, and marketable myths. If there are skeletons in the closet, they don't want you rattling them. They want you reciting affirmations and buying the boxed set.

But we're not here for the cartoon version. We're here for the raw, blood-and-bone truth. For the contradictions. For the shadows behind the spotlight. For the broken trail behind the myth.

Because Hill wasn't just a sage on the mountaintop. He was a hustler. A runaway. A failure. A man with lawsuits, shady business dealings, and more bankruptcies than bank accounts. He promised riches, but spent much of his life ducking debt collectors. He wrote about power but often lived on the edge of powerlessness. And yet... he left behind one of the most influential texts in the modern world.

That's the paradox. That's the uncomfortable, irresistible core of this story.

The reason this biography is unofficial is because the official story is stale. Sanitized. Safe. It tells you Hill had a conversation with Andrew Carnegie, got commissioned to write a 20-year success study, and emerged from the flames like Moses with stone tablets. But there's no hard evidence the Carnegie meeting ever happened. No documents. No diary entries. No witnesses. Just Hill's word—and Hill's word wasn't always gold.

That doesn't mean the whole thing's a fraud. But it does mean we need to treat the story like grown-ups. It means digging into the inconsistencies instead of ignoring them. It means looking past the poster and asking, Who was this guy, really? What kind of man preaches faith and prosperity while racking up failed ventures and courtroom drama?

The truth is: Hill's life was a mess. And that's what makes him worth studying.

Because if he'd been a polished titan, his words wouldn't matter. If he'd been perfect, he wouldn't be believable. His whole philosophy hinges on this dangerous, empowering idea: thoughts become things. But thoughts don't become yachts overnight. They become sweat, scars, bankruptcy notices, and breakthroughs. They become marriages, divorces, setbacks, and wild rebounds.

Hill lived that life.

Not the fantasy version. The real one. The version filled with contradiction. With pain. With chasing the vision and falling flat, again and again. But through it all, he never let go of the core belief: the mind is the forge, and every failure is just raw material.

What truths lie buried under Hill's mountain of success? This one: he was the embodiment of his own process. He didn't master the principles—he wrestled with them. He fell on his own sword more times than he'd probably admit. But that makes the sword real. It makes the lessons honest, even when the man wasn't.

The so-called experts who guard Hill's legacy want you to see the outcome, not the chaos that led there. They want the tidy quote, not the tangled context. But that's not what Hill was about—not if you read him right.

You can't think and grow rich unless you're willing to break and grow honest first. You can't manifest anything worthwhile without cutting through delusion and looking dead-on at your own flaws. Hill knew that. His whole life was one long, painful seminar in self-reinvention. And if he embellished his past, it was because he believed the myth would serve more people than the mess.

But here's the radical idea: maybe both matter. Maybe the myth and the mess are two sides of the same coin. Maybe the power of Hill's work is stronger when you realize he was one of us. Flawed. Flailing. Forging a path through failure with nothing but conviction and a typewriter.

So no, this isn't the version you'll hear at a corporate retreat. This is the back-alley biography. The unauthorized version. The one that tells you Hill wasn't just a messenger—he was the battlefield.

And that's why he matters. Not because he had all the answers, but because he refused to stop asking the question: What is a man capable of if he truly believes?

Even if the belief was sometimes a lie.

Even if the journey was a mess.

Even if the success was more myth than money.

This book is unofficial because truth doesn't wear a tie. It doesn't get rubber-stamped by a Foundation. It doesn't care about branding. It cares about meaning. And there's more meaning in the complicated Napoleon Hill than in the polished one.

If that's a hill worth dying on, so be it.

4

Early Life in Rural Virginia

Before Napoleon Hill became a prophet of wealth, he was dirt. Dirt poor, dirt covered, and born into the kind of isolation that either crushes a man or sharpens him to a blade. No silver spoons. No well-connected uncles. Just the backwoods of Wise County, Virginia, 1883—Appalachia at its most unforgiving.

This wasn't the South of Scarlett O'Hara and mint juleps. This was the South where coal dust choked your lungs and ambition was considered a disease. Where survival passed for success, and dreams were the kind of thing people laughed at—especially if you were the bastard son of an illiterate laborer.

Hill's mother died when he was nine. If that doesn't fracture something permanent in a boy, nothing will. His father remarried shortly after, and that's when the first spark lit. His stepmother, Martha, did something rare—she didn't write him off. She told him he wasn't a mistake. That his mind mattered. That the fire in his belly wasn't something to be beaten out of him like most boys in the holler. She gave him permission to want more. And that one act may have changed the course of millions of lives.

Because that's what Napoleon Hill became—an agent of more. But back then? He was just another kid with a gun, literally. By age 13, he was carrying a six-shooter, playing outlaw, and chasing stories of Jesse James and Billy the Kid. He wrote about it later like it was romantic. It wasn't. It was a broken kid in a broken place doing what broken boys do—trying to matter, trying to feel power in a world designed to rob him of it.

He started writing for small-town newspapers around 15. Not because he had a burning passion for journalism—but because it was a ticket out. The typewriter became his weapon. Words became currency. It was his first taste of influence, of being able to bend reality through articulation. That's something that never left him. The idea that if you could write it, you could live it.

But make no mistake—he wasn't some genius plucked from obscurity. He clawed for every inch. He hustled, lied, begged, and bartered his way into relevance. Early mentors weren't handing him opportunity—they were testing whether he'd survive long enough to deserve one. And Hill did, barely. There are no cute yearbook photos of him dreaming big in a cap and gown. There's just the grinding misery of rural poverty and a boy too smart to die in it.

The thing about Appalachia is it produces two kinds of men: the ones who get swallowed by the hills, and the ones who set them on fire on the way out. Hill wasn't content to leave. He wanted to conquer. Not the land—but the idea that the land defined him.

And that's the piece people miss when they look at Hill's later life and call him a charlatan. They see the polished words and forget the feral kid behind them. They mock the mysticism and forget the desperation. They forget what it costs to crawl out of a world that teaches you not to dream too loud.

Hill was born in a place that didn't just lack opportunity—it punished those who looked for it. And that punishment etched itself into him. It made him paranoid, proud, relentless, and sometimes dishonest. But it also made him powerful. Because once you've stared into the pit of irrelevance and refused to blink, no boardroom or billionaire intimidates you.

Rural Virginia didn't give Hill a foundation. It gave him a furnace. A forge. It burned away weakness, clarity, and comfort—and what walked out of that fire wasn't a saint. It was a man with a mission. A man willing to make himself into a myth if that's what it took to prove that your origins don't own you.

And that's the real legacy of his early years—not the trauma, not the loss, not even the grinding poverty. It's the defiance. The refusal. The unspoken war between where he came from and what he believed he could become.

You want to understand Napoleon Hill? Don't start with the books. Start with the boy. The one in the hills with no money, no map, and no mercy. The one who realized, way too early, that nobody was coming to save him—and decided that he'd build an empire instead.

Even if he had to lie a little to do it.

5

Poverty, Ambition, and Storytelling Roots

Napoleon Hill didn't just grow up poor—he grew up surrounded by poverty that knew no shame, no ceiling, and no expiration date. The kind of generational poverty that bakes into your bones and tells you it's normal. In the hills of Virginia, money wasn't even part of the conversation—it was a rumor. What mattered was whether you could feed yourself and avoid freezing to death. If you could do that, you were ahead of the curve.

Hill wasn't just hungry—he was humiliated. He hated being poor. Not in some abstract, noble, poetic sense. He despised it. He resented the dirt under his nails and the small-mindedness in the air. And it's that resentment that fueled his ambition. Hill didn't dream of making money—he dreamed of escaping irrelevance. That's a very different thing. He wasn't just trying to make a living. He was trying to make a mark.

And in a world where nobody around him had a map, he did what the smartest poor kids always do—he started telling stories.

That's where the seeds of his power were planted. Not in wealth, but in words. Hill learned early on that people listen when you make them feel something. And he had a gift for that. He knew how to frame struggle as suspense. How to turn hardship into narrative. Most kids in his shoes would sit quiet, ashamed of their station. Hill leaned in. He spun yarns. He dramatized. And eventually, he sold it.

Because the truth is, storytelling isn't just entertainment—it's survival. Especially for the poor. It's how you gain influence without money, how you negotiate without leverage, how you convince others (and yourself) that you matter. And Hill mastered that. He learned that if you could command a room, you didn't have to own it.

But there's a darker side to that gift. When you rely on storytelling to escape reality, the line between truth and fiction starts to blur. And in Hill's case, it blurred often. He didn't just stretch the truth—he sometimes broke it over his knee. His early accounts of interviews with Carnegie, Edison, and other titans often have no verifiable record. Critics call that fraud. But to Hill, it was narrative necessity.

He wasn't trying to report facts—he was trying to teach belief. He believed that belief itself was more powerful than biography. That if the story worked, if it ignited desire, then it was true enough. That mindset explains most of what Hill did with his life. He wasn't crafting memoirs. He was forging myths. Because he knew something most people don't: reality bends more easily to a good story than to a cold fact.

So poverty gave him ambition. And ambition forced him to weaponize narrative. He couldn't buy respect, so he earned attention. He couldn't build wealth, so he built the idea of wealth, and sold it with ferocity. People didn't follow Hill because he had millions. They followed him because he made them believe they could.

That's the hustle. That's the paradox. He sold the map while still wandering the woods himself. But that's what makes his legacy honest in a twisted, brilliant way. He was never preaching from the mountaintop. He was climbing with you—slipping, bullshitting, getting back up, and daring you to keep going.

Modern culture is quick to dismiss ambition as arrogance, or storytelling as manipulation. But that's just cowardice in disguise. Hill knew what the cowards couldn't admit: that greatness starts with wanting more than you're given, and being bold enough to say it out loud. Even if your hands are empty. Even if your bank account is a punchline.

His roots weren't polished. They were brutal. They were real. And they forced him to invent himself—piece by piece, word by word. If he hadn't been poor, he never would've developed the obsession. If he hadn't been surrounded by mediocrity, he never would've aimed so high. And if he hadn't learned to sell a story, he never would've made it past the coal mines.

He didn't escape poverty by luck. He escaped by conviction. And conviction, like hunger, doesn't lie.

So when you read Think and Grow Rich, understand this: it's not the polished work of a rich man giving back. It's the battle cry of a poor man who refused to die anonymous. Every sentence is laced with desperation, ambition, and the relentless force of someone who knew what it felt like to be counted out—and chose to rewrite the count.

6

Loss of His Mother, Influence of His Stepmother

When Napoleon Hill was just nine years old, death came into his house and shattered whatever fragile sense of normalcy existed. His mother, Sarah Sylvania Hill, died young—consumed by the hardship of Appalachian life and the brutal realities of childbirth and poverty. In a time and place where life was already cheap, her death could have been just another sad footnote.

But it wasn't.

It left a crater in Hill's soul, one that he carried for the rest of his life. That loss wasn't a chapter—it was a fault line. One that split his childhood in two. On one side was the innocent, dependent boy. On the other, the boy who had to figure out how to become a man before his voice even dropped.

He was left with his father, James Hill—a man not known for his warmth. The elder Hill was functional, not nurturing. He didn't raise Napoleon so much as keep him alive. Like most men of the time, especially in that hard land, he worked with his hands and expected the world to be simple: you eat, you work, you survive. Feelings? Irrelevant. Dreams? Dangerous. James didn't understand his son's mind—and maybe didn't care to. All he saw was a boy drifting toward trouble. A boy who needed discipline, not direction.

And Hill was drifting. His grief didn't make him quiet—it made him wild. He became angry. Rebellious. He started running around with a pistol and acting like the outlaw heroes he read about in pulp fiction. Not because he wanted to hurt anyone, but because it was the only version of male power he could understand. If the world takes your mother and gives you nothing in return, you start taking things back any way you can.

Then came Martha.

Hill's stepmother, Martha Ramey Banner, entered the picture when Napoleon was ten—and unlike most step-parent stories, this one didn't end in bitterness. It marked the beginning of something profound. Martha didn't see a delinquent. She saw a boy in pain. A boy with potential. A boy with fire—misdirected, yes, but burning bright underneath the rage.

She did something rare in Hill's world: she spoke to his mind. She told him he was smart. That he was meant for more. That he didn't have to become another coal miner or petty criminal. That he had a brain, and it was worth something. She introduced him to books. To ideas. She took the wildness in him and redirected it toward learning.

That moment—that belief—was Hill's origin story.

Forget Carnegie. Forget Think and Grow Rich. It started there. With one woman who didn't buy the story of his smallness. With one person who believed he could write his way out of the valley. Martha gave him permission to be ambitious, and that's all a kid like Hill needed. Once that door opened, he didn't just walk through it—he blew it off the hinges.

Her influence didn't just steer him away from a path of crime. It sparked the entire philosophy he'd later build his empire on: you become what you believe. That wasn't theory to Hill. It was personal history. If belief could reshape his future, then maybe it could do the same for millions of others.

So when he later preached about autosuggestion, about faith, about the power of thought to overcome circumstance—it wasn't abstract. It was the voice of a stepmother who dared to see more in a dirt-poor boy with nothing but anger and a pen.

The loss of his mother may have broken something in him. But the presence of his stepmother built something stronger over top of it. And that's why his work resonates so deeply—it doesn't come from a place of comfort. It comes from a place of emotional violence. From losing the most important person in your life and being saved not by a system or a school, but by someone who chose to believe in you for no reason other than love.

And there's power in that.

Martha didn't make Hill into a genius. She made him into a fighter. She handed him a different weapon. Not a pistol—but words. Not rebellion—but ambition. She taught him that success wasn't about brute force, but about mastering the self. And that lesson, planted early and deep, never left him.

So yes—Hill's later work often smells like mysticism, ego, and overcompensation. But underneath all that? Is a boy who lost his mother, nearly lost himself, and was dragged back to the light by one woman who saw him clearly. That's not a footnote. That's the foundation.

And if you want to understand Napoleon Hill, you don't just trace the money, the myths, or the manuscripts.

You trace it back to that ten-year-old boy in a log cabin, standing between two women—one buried in the ground, the other handing him a book—and realizing, for the first time, that life could be more than just survival.

It could be transformation.

7

Teenage Years as a Reporter

If Napoleon Hill had one gift that outpaced all the others, it wasn't discipline. It wasn't even ambition. It was access. And he earned that access not by birthright, not by inheritance, but by mastering the oldest hustle in America: he picked up a pen and learned how to ask the right questions.

In his teens, Hill became a reporter—first for small-town newspapers in the coal country of Virginia, then slowly inching toward bigger stories and bigger names. But don't imagine some neatly dressed intern with a press badge and a clean record. This was Hill the hustler, young and raw, running on charm and audacity. He didn't get gigs by waiting for someone to offer them. He pushed. He showed up. He wrote fast and talked faster. And once he got his foot in the door, he didn't just cover the town gossip—he went after titans.

He realized something powerful early on: if you want to learn the game, talk to the ones who are winning it. So while most teenagers were content to punch the clock or haul coal, Hill was chasing interviews. He was getting inside the minds of the successful. Not just to write about them—but to decode them. To steal their formulas. To figure out what made them tick.

This was no schoolboy project. It was war. Information was his battlefield, and every article was a weapon. His questions weren't fluffy. They were surgical. What did you believe before you made it? What habits did you kill off? How did you get your mind to obey your will?

That kind of reporting? That's not journalism. That's extraction. It's psychological espionage.

And it's also the seedbed of what would later become Think and Grow Rich. Most people think Hill sat down at age 50 and had a divine download. Wrong. The book is a culmination of decades of obsession. Of listening. Of deconstructing the mental architecture of powerful men. The interviews he conducted as a teenager—long before anyone knew his name—became the scaffolding for his later work.

He wasn't after gossip. He was after truth. But not the kind of truth the newspapers wanted. He wanted the internal stuff. The mental mechanics. He didn't care what deals were made— he cared why they were made. What gave a man the confidence to risk everything? What belief kept him going when others quit? What invisible forces separated success from collapse?

That was Hill's beat.

And he got good at it. He wasn't the most experienced. But he was relentless. He had a way of talking to people that bypassed their defenses. He flattered, but not obviously. He mirrored. He made powerful men feel like prophets. He gave them a stage, and they gave him gold.

He didn't write for accolades. He wrote for ammunition. Every quote was another piece of the puzzle. Every article was another lesson in the psychology of success. He wasn't just transcribing stories—he was sharpening his thesis. Even if he didn't know it yet, he was crafting a worldview.

But again, let's not pretend this was a clean rise. Hill wasn't above embellishing a résumé. He made claims that couldn't always be verified. His name wasn't yet synonymous with "truth." It was synonymous with hustle. And sometimes, that hustle went sideways.

There are accounts that he exaggerated his credentials. That he puffed up his interviews beyond what actually took place. That he played fast and loose with timelines and sources. But ask yourself: does that make him a fraud—or does that make him American?

He wasn't working for The New York Times. He wasn't fact-checked by committees. He was a teenage kid trying to write his way out of a system designed to keep him poor, small, and silent. If he blurred a few lines to build a bigger picture, it's because he knew where he was going—and reality just hadn't caught up yet.

And more importantly, the insight was real. The principles were sound. The minds he probed may not have always remembered the interviews, but the patterns he captured are timeless. Desire. Persistence. Decision. Belief. He was gathering the raw ore of greatness, and he'd spend the next two decades refining it into gold.

Hill's teenage years as a reporter weren't glamorous. They were gritty. Full of rejection, bad pay, and long hours. But they were also his laboratory. His apprenticeship. His crucible. He learned how to think like the rich long before he ever had a dime. And more importantly, he learned how to think like someone who refuses to stay poor.

That's what makes his early career matter. He wasn't just observing success—he was hunting it. He wasn't just a reporter—he was a reverse-engineer. And in that role, he found his calling—not to write the news, but to rewrite the narrative of what's possible for anyone mad enough to believe.

Early Writings and Connection to Business Leaders

Napoleon Hill didn't wait for the world to ask what he thought—he started writing like it already cared. That's the first move of any great self-made mind: act as if. Don't ask for permission. Don't wait for credentials. Just go. Hill did. And the writing—raw, unfiltered, urgent—became his first weapon in a war against smallness.

His earliest published work wasn't high art. It was practical. Punchy. Designed to catch the attention of anyone who still had a spark left in them after a 12-hour workday. He wrote about success, about ambition, about personal power. And he did it from the inside out—not as a millionaire dispensing advice from a penthouse, but as a hungry young man clawing for answers in a broken system.

It was this hunger that led to his connection with business leaders—not because he was in their circle, but because he forced his way into it.

Hill's biggest break came in the form of an opportunity to write a series of success profiles for Bob Taylor's Magazine, a national publication that mixed human interest with practical business lessons. It was the early 1900s. The country was industrializing, wealth was consolidating, and people were waking up to the fact that hard work alone wasn't enough. They wanted secrets. And Hill was more than happy to collect and sell them.

His job was simple: interview the greats, distill their wisdom, publish the blueprint. But there was nothing simple about getting those interviews. The magazine had a name, sure, but Hill was still just a kid with a pen and a dream. What he lacked in pedigree, he made up for in persuasion. And if that didn't work, he leaned on fiction. When he couldn't get in the front door, he made up a story about already being inside.

Some say that's where the Carnegie connection was born.

According to Hill, he interviewed Andrew Carnegie, the steel titan and self-made billionaire. Not only that—he claimed Carnegie gave him a secret mission: dedicate the next 20 years to interviewing the most successful men in the country, uncover the laws of success, and share them with the world. No contract. No payment. Just a handshake and a legacy-defining mission.

That story? Never verified. No record from Carnegie. No letters. No confirmation from family. Nothing but Hill's word.

So you have two choices: believe it, or call bullshit.

But here's the thing—you don't have to believe the Carnegie legend to understand what Hill actually did. Whether or not he had the formal blessing of the steel king, Hill spent the next two decades pushing his way into the rooms that shaped the American economy. He interviewed Thomas Edison. Alexander Graham Bell. Henry Ford. William Wrigley Jr. And even if some of those interviews were brief, embellished, or recreated from research, the result was real: Hill collected the DNA of power, wrapped it in narrative, and started writing the first real philosophy of achievement for the average man.

That's the key.

Hill wasn't writing for elites. He was writing for anyone who was sick of being powerless. For the man tired of watching other people win. For the woman tired of being told to stay in her lane. He wasn't offering privilege—he was offering strategy. And he got that strategy by studying the people who built empires from scratch.

His early writings—some of which formed the foundation for his massive Law of Success series—weren't just summaries of interviews.

They were pattern recognition machines. Hill wasn't interested in luck. He wanted to know why the successful kept winning. What mental levers they pulled. What habits they built. What thoughts they refused to entertain.

And the more he wrote, the clearer the picture became: success had laws. It wasn't random. It wasn't reserved for the few. It was available to anyone willing to think, act, and believe in alignment with those laws.

That message? Revolutionary. Because it meant that poverty was optional. That failure was a phase, not a destiny. And that the only thing standing between you and greatness was you.

His early writings gained traction. Not just with readers, but with future collaborators. People started to notice that Hill wasn't just another journalist—he was a translator of power. He made the language of the elite accessible to the masses. He took the psychology of billionaires and turned it into a creed for the broken.

That's what made his work magnetic.

Of course, this magnetism came at a cost. Hill was always walking the edge between inspiration and inflation. Between storytelling and myth-making. But that's what all visionaries do. They speak things into existence, even if reality hasn't caught up yet.

So whether or not Carnegie ever tapped Hill on the shoulder and commissioned a life's work, it doesn't change what Hill did. He built the bridge. He gathered the wisdom. He connected with the titans, learned their language, and then—more importantly—translated it into something that could change your life.

That was the real miracle of his early career.

He didn't just write about the rich.

He wrote for the poor, the stuck, the broken, the pissed off, and the willing.

And he gave them the one thing poverty never hands out: a system.

9

Developing His Personal Philosophy

Napoleon Hill didn't sit down one day and invent a personal philosophy out of thin air. He reverse-engineered it from the minds of the men who had bent the world to their will. Not by theory. Not by armchair speculation. By asking direct, piercing questions to the most dangerous minds of the age—and listening like his life depended on it. Because it did.

These weren't puff interviews. They weren't lifestyle features or ego flattery pieces. They were recon missions. Hill walked into those rooms with one goal: to find out what the hell these men knew that everyone else didn't. And once he got even a glimpse, he didn't just write it down. He absorbed it. He digested it. He let it burn in his brain until the patterns started to surface.

That's when the philosophy started to take shape.

Hill wasn't interested in external strategy. He wasn't compiling business tips or financial hacks. He went straight for the source code: the inner world. What thoughts created results? What beliefs preceded achievement? What invisible decisions gave birth to empires?

Over time, the interviews became more than reporting. They became a form of psychological pattern recognition. Hill noticed that no matter what field these men dominated—industry, science, invention, banking—they all carried the same internal weapons: a definiteness of purpose, unshakable faith, obsessive focus, and a deep, visceral belief that their mind was the master key.

That's what hit Hill like a revelation. Not one of them credited luck. Not one of them leaned on circumstance. They expected success. Demanded it. They acted like the outcome was already written—they just had to live into it. This wasn't optimism. It was a form of mental aggression. And it changed the way Hill thought about thought itself.

He realized success wasn't the result of chance, or even raw talent. It was the result of alignment—between thought, desire, and action. The people who won weren't the smartest. They were the most intentional. They didn't hope. They decided. That was the big word. Decision. The capacity to decide what you wanted, decide you would get it, and decide never to stop until reality bent to your will.

That wasn't a motivational slogan for Hill. That was law. And the more he studied, the more the laws stacked up.

Out of those interviews came what would eventually be framed as Hill's famous 13 principles of success. Not because he sat in a quiet room and brainstormed them—but because he saw them over and over again, across dozens of powerful lives. Every man had his own tools, his own methods—but they all echoed the same truths: desire is fuel, faith is force, imagination is blueprint, persistence is armor, and the mind is the forge.

This was Hill's real breakthrough—not just that thoughts shape outcomes, but that thoughts, when deliberately and repeatedly focused, become magnetic. He didn't mean this in a woo-woo, incense-burning way. He meant it like gravity. You become what you dwell on. You attract what you expect. You create what you visualize and believe.

And he didn't just witness this. He tested it. On himself. Constantly.

He took what he learned in interviews and ran personal experiments. He observed his own failures, his depressions, his bankruptcies, and tried to map them against what he should've been thinking. Then he adjusted. Reframed. Reprogrammed. He was his own lab rat.

That's what most people miss when they read Think and Grow Rich and try to reduce it to platitudes. Hill wasn't theorizing from the stands. He was bleeding on the field. He failed, regrouped, and tried again. Over and over. Not because he was a masochist—but because he knew the rules were real. He had seen them work. He just had to keep learning how to obey them.

His interviews taught him that success wasn't magical—but it also wasn't mechanical. It required mental discipline. Something most people avoid like the plague. It's easier to blame the system, the market, the politicians. But Hill's interviews made one thing brutally clear: the successful blamed themselves. They took ownership of every outcome. Good, bad, or brutal. And that mindset became the backbone of Hill's personal philosophy.

It also made him dangerous.

Because once you believe that thought creates reality, the excuses start to die. And with them, all the institutions built on managing your failure. That's why Hill's message, to this day, exists in the margins. It's quoted, but rarely taught. It's praised, but rarely practiced. Because if it's true, then most people are the architects of their own misery. And most people aren't ready to handle that.

Hill was. And he wanted to show others how to be, too.

That's what he developed—not just a philosophy of success, but a philosophy of sovereignty. The idea that your mind is the throne room, and you either rule it—or get ruled by your fears, doubts, and programming. The men he interviewed had mastered that inner kingdom. Hill's life became a blueprint for how to get there yourself.

The interviews weren't the end. They were the beginning. The spark that lit a fire under a man who refused to die a nobody.

10

The Alleged 20-Year Assignment

No Paper Trail: Analyzing the Credibility

If you believe Napoleon Hill's version of the story, it all started with a single conversation that changed everything. A moment in time where fate handed him a mission. According to Hill, steel magnate Andrew Carnegie invited him to his estate, sat him down, and laid out a challenge that would shape the next two decades of his life.

Hill claimed Carnegie said this: "I want you to commit twenty years of your life to studying the most successful men in America, distilling their principles, and creating a philosophy of personal achievement that can uplift the common man."

No contract. No salary. Just a stopwatch placed silently on the desk. According to Hill, Carnegie gave him 60 seconds to decide whether or not to take the assignment.

He said yes, of course. That moment became the cornerstone of the Napoleon Hill mythology. The origin story. The spark that set fire to the whole movement.

But here's the problem: there's no proof it ever happened.

No letters. No references in Carnegie's archives. No photos, telegrams, or meeting records. No contemporary mention of Hill in Carnegie's extensive network of collaborators, secretaries, or associates. Just Hill's word—and Hill's word, as history shows, was sometimes flexible.

So, what do we do with this?

The skeptics are quick to slam the door: If there's no paper trail, it didn't happen. Hill was a liar. A fabulist. A grifter who made up the Carnegie story to wrap himself in borrowed credibility. That's the mainstream take in academic circles—and it's not without merit.

But here's the other side: maybe the story isn't meant to be factual. Maybe it was Hill's way of creating a narrative container powerful enough to hold the weight of what he was trying to build. Maybe it was mythology with purpose.

And that leads to a bigger question—what does this myth actually tell us?

What the Myth Says About Hill—and About Us
Whether Carnegie commissioned Hill or not almost becomes irrelevant when you realize how potent the idea is. Strip away the historicity, and you're left with a metaphor that still punches like a freight train:

A poor, untested young man is given a divine mission by one of the world's richest industrialists—to study success, decode its laws, and bring them to the masses.

That's not history. That's scripture.

And it tells you everything you need to know about Hill's genius—and his audience.

The truth is, Hill understood narrative power better than most authors ever will. He knew that people don't just want information—they want meaning. They want origin stories. They want the chosen one. They want to believe that greatness isn't reserved for the elite, but granted to anyone brave enough to say yes to destiny.

In that light, the Carnegie tale wasn't just a personal anecdote. It was a mirror. A parable meant to reflect your own possibility. Hill put himself in the role of the everyman—broke, hungry, unproven—and showed you that with the right mindset, the right questions, and the right purpose, you too could rise from obscurity and shape your reality.

Was it true? Probably not in the literal sense.

But was it useful? Absolutely.

And that's Hill in a nutshell. He was never selling facts. He was selling agency. He was saying, "If I can talk to titans, so can you. If I can build a philosophy, so can you. If I can rise from nothing, what's stopping you?"

The Carnegie story says more about Hill's understanding of belief systems than it does about his resume. He knew that humans are hardwired to follow archetypes. He cast himself as the disciple. The gatherer of wisdom. The bridge between the gods of industry and the people in the trenches. He didn't need a payroll stub—he needed a myth powerful enough to inspire movement.

And it worked.

Millions believed it. Still do. Because we want to believe that success can be systematized. That there's a key, a path, a secret—and that someone has taken the time to figure it out for the rest of us. The story didn't just elevate Hill—it activated his readers. It gave them a mission of their own.

But here's the dangerous side: once you accept the myth blindly, you lose the nuance. You start to expect your own "Carnegie moment." You wait for some titan to anoint you, to bless your mission, to confirm your purpose. You forget that Hill wrote the assignment for himself. That's the real lesson. He didn't wait to be validated. He created the narrative that gave him power.

That's what separates the passive from the powerful.

Hill's real genius wasn't in what he documented—it was in what he declared. He didn't just record success stories—he built a framework that others could step into. He created a space for belief. And for many, that belief was the first step toward personal transformation.

So, is the Carnegie story true?

It doesn't matter.

What matters is that Hill had the balls to speak it into existence—and then live like it was real. He wrote his own commission. He placed the stopwatch on his desk. He gave himself the assignment. And then he went out and did it.

That's not fraud.
That's fire.

11

Early Publications

Before there was Think and Grow Rich, there was The Law of Success. And before that, there was Hill's Golden Rule Magazine. These weren't bestsellers. They were battlegrounds—early prototypes of the gospel Hill was still figuring out how to preach. And like all first drafts, they were messy, raw, and full of ambition that outran their polish.

But they were also dangerous. Because they revealed what Hill was really trying to do: not just teach success, but build a movement. Not a feel-good club. A philosophical revolt against the idea that you were stuck with the hand life dealt you.

Let's start with Hill's Golden Rule Magazine.

Launched in 1919, it was Hill's first real attempt to become more than a writer. He wanted to be a thought leader, long before that term was corrupted by LinkedIn bios. The magazine was a mash-up of success stories, moral preaching, self-help principles, and early iterations of the ideas he'd refine later. Its tagline said it all: "Do unto others as you would have them do unto you." Sounds quaint now. But Hill meant it as a strategic command, not a sentimental one.

The deeper message of the magazine wasn't about manners. It was about power. Hill believed that ethical conduct and material success weren't enemies—they were allies. That you could win and do it with integrity. And he was desperate to prove it in print.

But desperation makes you vulnerable.

Hill's Golden Rule Magazine fell apart after just two years. Financial problems. Mismanagement. Accusations of shady deals. Some say Hill exaggerated circulation numbers. Some say he got swindled himself. Either way, it crashed. Hard. And Hill's name took a hit.

But like any true believer in his own myth, Hill didn't fold. He pivoted.

Out of the wreckage came The Law of Success, his 1,000+ page monster of a book, published in 1928. This wasn't a self-help pamphlet. It was a manual for world domination—spiritual, mental, and financial. It was the first time Hill laid out his now-famous philosophy in full, Frankenstein-like detail. Thirteen principles. Dozens of case studies. A roadmap from failure to fortune that pulled no punches.

And make no mistake—Hill didn't write this thing for the casual reader. He wrote it for the man who was done playing small. It was long, dense, and aggressive. Every chapter was a challenge: Are you serious about changing your life, or just looking for motivational candy?

The book didn't just teach mindset—it taught warfare. Mental warfare. Strategic belief. The power of definiteness. The necessity of burning bridges to force progress. Hill wrapped up capitalism, mysticism, and personal development into a single unified theory of human potential—and then dropped it like a bomb.

But like every bomb, it had collateral damage.

The success of The Law of Success was modest at first. The economy was about to collapse, and Hill's publishing partners weren't all saints. He found himself betrayed, broke again, and on the move. For every opportunity he created, a lawsuit seemed to follow. For every philosophical breakthrough, there was a financial beatdown. That's the story no one likes to tell: that the man writing the rules was still learning to live by them.

But here's the truth: The Law of Success wasn't a failure. It was a blueprint. Everything Hill would later refine into Think and Grow Rich was here, hidden beneath a mountain of words. All the greats have an early work that doesn't catch fire until long after they're gone. This was

Hill's. Raw. Overstuffed. Brilliant. And too much for the public at the time.

So what did Hill do? He went leaner. Sharper. More focused. He distilled the message, cut the fat, and prepped for a second strike. But even in these early books, you can see the bones of a revolution. You see a man who believed—truly believed—that success could be taught like geometry or chemistry. That anyone with the right mix of burning desire, focus, and persistence could escape the mediocrity factory and take back control of their destiny.

Of course, Hill's critics love to point out that while he was writing about success, he was often broke, unemployed, or on the run. But that's exactly why his work hits harder. He wasn't preaching from a palace. He was fighting for his life. Writing from the trenches. And still, he believed. That's not hypocrisy. That's conviction under fire.

And that's the real story of Hill's early publications.

They weren't commercial triumphs.

They were ideological detonations.

The first shots of a lifelong war against helplessness.

And if they didn't all sell, if they didn't all stick the landing, that's fine.

Because revolutions don't begin with applause.

They begin with a man willing to write the truth before the world is ready to read it.

12

Lawsuits, Bankruptcy, and Accusations

S uccess stories are always cleaner after the mess is scrubbed from the record. But Napoleon Hill's record? It bleeds. Not just with setbacks, but with courtrooms, creditors, broken contracts, and broken promises. He didn't just struggle—he staggered, crashed, and got dragged into accusations that would've buried most men.

But Hill didn't die. He adapted. And he used every failure like a forge.

Let's talk about the parts the Napoleon Hill Foundation likes to skip. The legal filings. The unpaid debts. The double-crossed investors. The business partners left holding the bag while Hill skipped town and started over under a new name or in a new city.

Hill's reputation as a man of success was built during an era when fact-checking was slow and trust was transactional. And he took full advantage. He didn't lie so much as frame reality to his advantage. If a deal failed, it was someone else's fault. If a venture collapsed, the market wasn't ready. If money disappeared, it was an unfortunate consequence of ambition.

But when the paper trail is examined, it's not just one or two hiccups. It's a pattern.

Let's start with the magazine debacle—Hill's Golden Rule. By the time it folded, lawsuits had already started flying. Hill was accused of misrepresenting circulation numbers to lure investors. Money disappeared. Salaries went unpaid. Promises made under the golden banner of ethics turned to ash. One suit after another was filed. Most were quietly dismissed or settled—often with Hill simply vanishing from town.

That was his move: escape and reinvention.

But the pattern followed him.

In the 1920s, he launched multiple businesses—schools, training centers, publishing projects—all with big visions, big words, and bad follow-through. More investors. More optimism. More flames. One such venture, a success school in Chicago, promised business leadership training based on his growing success principles. It collapsed before graduating a class. Lawsuit.

By 1923, Hill filed for bankruptcy. Not just once—multiple times. The details are muddy, but the impact was real. He had more debt than assets. His name was poisoned in professional circles. And still, he moved forward like none of it happened. He kept writing, kept teaching, kept telling the world that thoughts become things—even if his thoughts were producing IOUs.

Critics say this makes him a con man. A fraud. A preacher of wealth who couldn't pay rent. And they're not wrong—at least, not on paper.

But let's press deeper.

What kind of man keeps writing about faith in the middle of financial ruin? What kind of man stares down the humiliation of public failure and still insists that mindset is stronger than circumstance?

That's not fraud. That's belief so feral it survives public execution.

Hill didn't just believe in his philosophy—he was testing it in real time, under fire. And yeah, sometimes that meant crossing moral lines. He overpromised. He underdelivered. He made bold claims and didn't back them up. He convinced people to invest in projects that never launched, and he used charisma to cover operational incompetence.

But you have to ask yourself—was he scamming the world, or trying to convince it before he convinced himself?

Because here's the gut punch: Hill's greatest fraud may have been against his own fear. His life was a bet. A bet that if he acted like the man he wanted to be, the universe would eventually catch up. And sometimes it did. Most of the time, it didn't. But he never stopped betting.

That's what makes him dangerous. And inspiring. And, yeah—divisive.

The lawsuits didn't stop him.

The bankruptcies didn't stop him.

Even when people called him a fraud to his face, Hill never flinched. Because he wasn't building a brand. He was building a reality. He knew that success is messy. Ugly. That most great men go broke before they go big. And he believed that if you quit when the world accuses you, you were never worthy of the prize anyway.

That's the dark brilliance of Hill. He didn't just write about risk—he lived it. If you want a clean role model, look elsewhere. Hill was chaos. He was contradiction. But inside that storm, he was also free.

Free from waiting for approval. Free from playing by the rules of the cautious. Free from the need to be liked, understood, or even believed.

Yes—he failed.

Yes—he got sued.

Yes—he built castles on sand and convinced others to live in them.

But he also wrote a book that changed millions of lives, while broke, battered, and widely doubted. And that's the inconvenient truth: fraud or not, the system he taught works—if you're brave enough to use it.

In a world full of cowards who hide behind credentials and excuses, Hill did what most won't: he believed himself into being.

And that belief, whatever else you want to call it, was not fake.

It was ferocious.

13

Building a Philosophy Through Hardship

Napoleon Hill didn't write his philosophy in a study lined with gold-leaf books while sipping bourbon from a leather chair. He wrote it while drowning. While broke. While failing. Again and again. He built it not as a monument to wealth, but as a lifeline out of collapse. The foundation of Think and Grow Rich wasn't prosperity—it was pain.

That's what most people miss.

They see the polished quotes, the success seminars, the cherry-picked bios. They think Hill had it all figured out, that he tapped into some divine frequency and rode the wave into fortune and fame. But the truth is messier. Darker. And far more valuable.

Hill built his philosophy the same way a soldier sharpens a knife in a trench—because he had to. Because nothing else worked. Because the world didn't hand him anything but problems. And instead of collapsing, he chose to interpret his suffering as feedback.

Every principle he taught was forged in failure.

Desire? Hill knew what it felt like to want something so badly it hurt. He knew how it gnawed at you when the bills were overdue, the lights were shut off, and the world didn't care what was in your heart. He learned early that shallow desires got blown away by the first storm—but a burning desire, one that claws its way into your bones, can survive anything.

Faith? Not church-on-Sunday faith. Not empty platitudes. Hill's faith was forged in silence—when no one believed in him, when his ventures tanked, when the lawsuits piled up and every path forward was blocked. It was the kind of faith that doesn't ask for evidence—it creates it. The kind of faith that says, "I'm going to win," even while packing up another failure and fleeing town.

Persistence? Hill's entire life was persistence. Bankruptcy didn't stop him. Public shame didn't stop him. He failed as an editor, failed as a businessman, failed as a speaker. His relationships collapsed. His finances were a mess. But he kept moving. Kept writing. Kept building. Because he understood something most people never learn: quitting is more comfortable than failing repeatedly—but only failure sharpens the edge of success.

Even autosuggestion—Hill's infamous mind-reprogramming method—wasn't some esoteric ritual. It was a survival tool. When the world screamed "you're done," Hill needed a louder voice in his own head screaming, "you're just getting started." That wasn't philosophy. That was psychological warfare. He needed to convince himself every single day that his thoughts still mattered, even when his reality said otherwise.

Hill's philosophy didn't come from comfort. It came from confrontation. He looked his failures in the face and refused to believe they were final. He interrogated them. He asked: What is this teaching me? Where did I give up responsibility? What thought led to this outcome? And then he turned those lessons into doctrine.

The average person breaks under hardship. Hill took hardship and said, this is the curriculum. Pain was the classroom. Failure was the textbook. His whole life was one long PhD in suffering—and instead of letting it define him, he mined it for principles.

And that's what makes his philosophy dangerous.

Because it doesn't coddle. It doesn't offer safe spaces or shortcuts. It demands ownership. If your life is a mess, Hill doesn't tell you to go to therapy and process your trauma. He tells you to take the wheel and burn your excuses. He tells you that every problem is a reflection of your thinking—and that until you change your mind, you'll keep repeating the same disaster with a different name.

That's not gentle. It's not palatable. But it's true.

Because Hill lived it.

He didn't invent the 13 principles from a place of success. He crawled through hell, wrote them down in the ashes, and dared you to try them. Not when life is easy—but when life is ripping you apart. That's where they work. That's where they become real.

Hill wasn't a guru. He was a fighter. A man backed into corners so many times he stopped looking for exits and started punching through walls. His success wasn't the result of knowing the right people—it was the result of not giving up when everyone else would have.

That's the real philosophy.

Not some intellectual theory.

But a weapon.

A fire-forged set of beliefs that turn hardship into heat and heat into momentum.

So the next time someone quotes Hill with a smile and a coffee cup, remember: those words weren't born in peace. They were born in war. And they're not motivational slogans. They're survival strategies for anyone with the guts to stop waiting for miracles and start building them in the dark.

14

Think and Grow Rich – The Cult Classic

The 1937 Release and Its Impact

Think and Grow Rich dropped in 1937 like a bomb—and the blast radius is still being measured today. This wasn't just a book release. It was a quiet revolution disguised as a self-help manual. A counter-punch to the Great Depression. A blueprint for the man or woman sick of waiting for permission to succeed.

Hill didn't just write a book. He gave people a weapon.

The timing was surgical. America was bleeding. Families crushed by the collapse of the markets, the farms, the factories. Dreams dissolved in bread lines. And here comes this thin, bold book whispering something no one else was saying out loud: your mind is still sovereign. Your thoughts still matter. And the world doesn't get the final say—you do.

That message hit like a drug.

People weren't buying Think and Grow Rich because it was clever. They were buying it because it gave them back agency. It wasn't senti-mental. It was sharp. Strategic. Hill's tone wasn't sympathetic—it was demanding. He didn't coddle his reader. He challenged them. And they responded by the millions.

Let's be clear: Hill didn't invent personal development. But he weaponized it.

The book sold slowly at first. Word of mouth carried it like wildfire. It didn't need marketing—it had a message so potent, people passed it around like contraband. Within a decade, it was everywhere. Translated, reprinted, bootlegged, quoted. And it didn't stop with sales—it started changing lives. For real. Because Hill wasn't selling motivation. He was selling a system.

Thirteen principles.

Not theory. Law.

Desire. Faith. Autosuggestion. Specialized Knowledge. Imagination. Organized Planning. Decision. Persistence. Power of the Master Mind. The Mystery of Sex Transmutation. The Subconscious Mind. The Brain. The Sixth Sense.

Each one a blade. Together—a full arsenal.

And here's the trick: Hill didn't just lay them out. He commanded you to apply them. He told you to burn your excuses, focus your mind like a laser, and get to war with your own mediocrity. This wasn't a how-to guide for gentle improvement. It was a manifesto for psychological insurgency.

The result?

A cult following. Not in the weird-robes-and-rituals sense, but in the original meaning of the word: a movement centered around a shared belief system. Think and Grow Rich wasn't just read—it was lived. Businessmen swore by it. Salesmen memorized it. Athletes applied it. Hustlers evangelized it. For every skeptic, there were a dozen people pointing to their copy like a compass that got them out of the woods.

And it didn't stop with individuals. The book reshaped entire industries.

Corporate America built training systems around it. Sales organizations adopted it like scripture. Motivational speaking as a business model exists because Hill made belief into a product. Every time you hear a guru tell you to visualize, to believe, to take massive action—you're hearing echoes of 1937.

But the impact wasn't just material.

Hill's book infected culture with a deeper idea: that wealth was not a sin, and that desire was not shameful. That alone flipped the moral programming of generations raised to believe poverty was noble and ambition was dangerous. Hill smashed that illusion. He reframed desire as the engine of all progress.

And yes—he included spiritual overtones. He wasn't shy about invoking the subconscious, infinite intelligence, or the sixth sense. But he didn't preach. He dared. He said, "There's more power inside you than you've been told, and if you don't access it, you've got no one to blame but yourself."

That's why the book endures.

Because Hill didn't promise comfort. He promised control. Not over the economy. Not over politics. Over your own damn mind. And in a world addicted to victimhood and distraction, that's heresy. But heresy has always been the birthplace of freedom.

Think and Grow Rich became a cult classic not because it was flawless—but because it was fearless. It was blunt. Bold. And it refused to let you off the hook. The title alone was a slap in the face. Not Work Hard and Grow Rich. Not Save and Invest and Grow Rich. Think. Your thoughts are the soil. Your beliefs are the seed. Your outcome is your harvest—or your famine.

And if you're broke? Look inward. Not outward.

That's the core of Hill's impact.

He didn't sell hope. He sold responsibility.

And that's why this book still sits on desks, in backpacks, and in the hands of men and women about to break something wide open.

Because when you're ready to stop waiting, and start building from the inside out—Hill's book is still there.

Still daring.

Still dangerous.

Still undefeated.

Core Principles of the Book

Napoleon Hill didn't write Think and Grow Rich to impress any-one. He wrote it to provoke you. To challenge you. To slap you awake from the trance of mediocrity. At the core of the book are 13 prin-ciples—his so-called "Philosophy of Achievement." But don't let the word "philosophy" fool you. These aren't suggestions. These are weapons. Rules for war. A mental operating system for those who are done playing small.

Let's break them down—not like a textbook, but like a blueprint for taking your power back.

1. Desire

Hill opens with a truth most people are too afraid to admit: you have to want something before you can get it. Not casually. Not politely. Obses-sively. He calls it a "burning desire"—a want so white-hot it incinerates fear, laziness, and doubt.

Desire isn't wishful thinking. It's decision with teeth. You either want it bad enough to rearrange your life, or you don't want it at all. Most people confuse wanting with whining. Hill didn't.

2. Faith

Not religion. Not tradition. Faith in yourself. Faith in your vision. Faith that your goal already exists in potential form—and that your job is to align your mind with that reality until it becomes physical.

Hill says faith is cultivated through repetition. You program it. You create it by force, through autosuggestion, until your subconscious ac-cepts it as fact. And once that happens? Your actions change. Your ex-pectations change. And your results follow suit.

3. Autosuggestion

The mind doesn't care if something is true. It cares if it's repeated. That's the basis of autosuggestion—the act of feeding your mind the be-liefs you choose until they replace the ones you were programmed with.

You're already being hypnotized by the media, by your parents, by your environment. Hill's point? Hypnotize yourself on purpose. Feed your mind thoughts of power, wealth, and courage. Do it daily. Make it a ritual. And eventually, your subconscious will act on what it's been told.

4. Specialized Knowledge

Degrees don't matter. Knowledge is only power when it's applied. Hill makes it clear: general education produces employees. Specialized knowledge—focused, actionable, relevant—is what builds empires.

If you want to win, you need to know something others don't. Or do something others won't. You don't need to know everything. You need to become lethal at one thing—and use that to create leverage.

5. Imagination

Imagination isn't fantasy. It's creation. It's the ability to see what doesn't yet exist and believe in it hard enough to build it. Hill separates it into two types: synthetic and creative. Synthetic draws from existing ideas. Creative taps into something deeper—what he calls Infinite Intelligence.

Every invention, every business, every revolution started in someone's mind. That's not poetry. That's physics.

6. Organized Planning

Desire without a plan is masturbation. Hill knew that. You need action steps. You need logistics. You need clarity. And most importantly—you need to adapt. Hill warns that your first plan will likely fail. That's not defeat. That's data.

He tells you to fail forward. To revise. To re-strategize. The planning isn't what matters—it's your refusal to stop planning until something works.

7. Decision

Indecision is death. The rich decide fast and change slow. The poor decide slow and change fast. That's one of Hill's hardest pills to swallow—but one of the most accurate.

Success requires commitment. Momentum. You can't tiptoe into greatness. You declare it. You move. You adapt after you've already burned the ships.

8. Persistence

Persistence is Hill's word for grit. Not enthusiasm. Not effort. The refusal to give up when your ego is bruised, your bank is empty, and your friends are laughing behind your back.

Most people stop when they hit resistance. Hill's whole thesis is that resistance is the proof you're on the right path. And if you persist long enough, the wall cracks.

9. Power of the Master Mind

No one wins alone. Hill says power is the result of organized knowledge directed by two or more minds working in harmony toward a shared goal. That's the Master Mind.

This isn't networking. This is mental alliance. A high-trust, high-intensity connection with people who elevate you, challenge you, and keep you accountable. If you're surrounded by losers, you lose. If you're surrounded by killers, you sharpen.

10. The Mystery of Sex Transmutation

This is where Hill gets metaphysical—and most people skip the chapter because they're not ready.

Hill believed that sexual energy is the strongest creative force known to man. But left unchanneled, it's a distraction. Redirected, it becomes ambition. He wasn't anti-sex—he was pro-power. He said the great men of history learned to convert that drive into creative output, business success, and visionary execution.

Modern society sells sex as a hobby. Hill saw it as a rocket fuel most people waste on porn and parties.

11. The Subconscious Mind

Your subconscious is always listening. Always recording. Always reacting to what you really believe—not what you say out loud, but what you accept internally.

Hill's warning: if you feed it fear, it will multiply fear. If you feed it belief, it will bend reality around that belief. Your subconscious doesn't judge. It acts. And your job is to become the programmer, not the victim of programming.

12. The Brain

To Hill, the brain wasn't just a thinking organ—it was a broadcasting station. A receiver. A transmitter. He believed that thoughts were not confined to the skull—they radiated out, attracted their match, and returned as circumstances.

You don't have to buy the radio-wave metaphor. But the real point is this: your mind affects more than you can see. The mental becomes physical. The invisible becomes visible. Thought is the seed. Results are the fruit.

13. The Sixth Sense

Hill ends with mystery. He admits this principle can't be taught—it must be experienced. The sixth sense is intuition. It's alignment. It's the moment when all the principles click into place and you start operating with instinct instead of effort.

It's flow. It's grace. It's power without push.

Most never get there. Because most never do the work required by the other twelve principles.

These principles aren't fluff. They're not Pinterest quotes. They're a system. And systems work when you work them. Hill didn't just pull this stuff out of thin air. He extracted it from the most successful minds of his time—and then lived it, bled for it, and demanded that you apply it.

One principle at a time.

Until your thoughts stop being dreams...

...and start becoming evidence.

15

Stories of Transformation (Real and Imagined)

Think and Grow Rich didn't just sell books—it sold identity. It gave the broke man a throne. It gave the lost woman a compass. It told people they weren't stuck, weren't broken, weren't bound to the life they'd been dealt. And people didn't just believe it—they proved it, or at least claimed to.

Hill's work created a tidal wave of testimonials—some real, some imagined, and some that walked a razor's edge between inspiration and delusion. But that's the thing about transformation: it doesn't always look clean. It doesn't come with receipts. It comes with conviction.

Let's start with the real.

Hill's book is directly credited by countless entrepreneurs, millionaires, athletes, and thinkers as the moment their life flipped. People like:

Daymond John, founder of FUBU and star of Shark Tank, who says Think and Grow Rich taught him the discipline to rise from hustling in Queens to building a fashion empire.

Bob Proctor, who built an entire career—and his own self-help empire—off the back of Hill's principles, teaching mindset to millions before "mindset coaching" was a thing.

Jim Carrey, who wrote himself a $10 million check when he was broke, citing Hill's principles of visualization and belief. A decade later, he cashed it in with Dumb and Dumber.

Oprah Winfrey referenced Hill's teachings indirectly for years—championing belief, responsibility, and visualization as the keys to success.

These aren't coincidences. These are people who read Hill, applied it, and went from obscurity to orbit. They didn't treat the book as inspiration—they treated it as a manual. That's the difference.

But Hill didn't stop at case studies. He also told stories. And that's where the line between truth and truth-shaped fiction gets blurry.

There's the story of a deaf-mute boy—Hill's own son—whom he claims learned to hear through the application of desire, faith, and autosuggestion. Doctors said the child would never hear, never speak, never function. Hill refused to accept it. He fed the boy belief. And according to Hill, not only did the child learn to hear—he later worked for a hearing aid company and inspired thousands of others with hearing loss.

That story sits at the emotional core of Think and Grow Rich. It's powerful. Raw. But skeptics have poked at the details. Did the boy's hearing return naturally? Was Hill's version of the events dramatized? Probably. But that's not the point. The function of the story is what matters. It shows that transformation, even in the face of hopeless odds, starts with mindset. Not medicine. Not miracles. Belief.

Then there's the story of Edwin C. Barnes—the man who "thought himself into a partnership with Thomas Edison." Hill paints a picture of a broke nobody stepping off a freight train, declaring his intention to work with Edison, and refusing to leave until the universe complied.

The story is iconic. But here's the catch: details are scarce. Some records suggest Barnes was indeed connected to Edison. Others suggest Hill took creative liberties. Either way, the message is clear: desire + action + refusal to quit = results.

Hill's world is full of these tales. Some provable. Some poetic. And yes, some probably bullshit. But that's the cost of playing in the space between psychology and faith. You have to accept that some transformations happen in secret. They don't show up on a spreadsheet. They show up in a man's posture. In his choices. In the fact that he used to work for someone else and now signs his own damn checks.

And even if some stories are exaggerated, that doesn't make the transformations they triggered any less real. Because belief doesn't require evidence—it creates it.

That's the genius of Hill's work. He knew that people needed examples, not just instruction. They needed stories to step into, mirrors to see themselves in, lives to model their own after. And if the facts needed a little help to drive the point home, so be it. Hill wasn't a historian. He was a strategist for the soul.

But don't think for a second it was all fairy tales. Some transformations were gritty, brutal, and real. Like the man who read Hill while in prison, applied the principles, and came out to build a multi-million dollar business. Or the single mother who used the book to fuel her way through school, start her company, and break a cycle of generational poverty.

These people exist. Quietly. Without fanfare. But ask them what flipped the switch and they'll hand you a beat-up copy of Hill's book like it's a holy relic.

Because that's what it became.

Think and Grow Rich wasn't a self-help book. It was a transformation trigger. For some, it changed their net worth. For others, their identity. But in every case, the power came not from the paper—but from the application.

And that's where most people fail.

They read. They nod. They highlight. And then... they do nothing.

Hill's book only works if you do. You have to decide. You have to burn the bridge. You have to become the story of transformation, not just consume one.

And if you do?

You stop living as a witness to other people's success...

...and you become the next unbelievable story someone else can't wait to retell.

16

Hill's Flirtation with Mysticism

For a guy whose name became synonymous with gritty, practical self-improvement, Napoleon Hill spent a lot of time in the clouds. Not metaphorically. Literally. He wrote about something he called "Infinite Intelligence," accessed his so-called "Invisible Counselors" in nightly mind rituals, and insisted that thoughts could travel through the ether—a metaphysical force field of human intention and imagination.

Yeah. It got weird.

And here's the thing: Hill never apologized for any of it.

He didn't care if it made the academics squirm or the business guys roll their eyes. To him, this was the source code of success. All the external wins—money, position, respect—they were downstream from something bigger. Something unseen. And while most people just wanted the checklist, Hill kept pointing back to the sky and saying, you're missing the power if you can't feel the frequency.

Let's start with autosuggestion—Hill's foundational technique for programming the subconscious mind. It wasn't optional. It was mandatory. In fact, if you don't grasp autosuggestion, you don't understand Hill at all.

Autosuggestion is simple in theory and violent in practice: you speak what you want into your mind until your mind starts making it real. Not once. Not when you feel like it. Relentlessly. Morning. Night. With emotion. With urgency. Until the belief takes root so deep it overpowers every doubt and every external piece of evidence to the contrary.

Hill didn't come up with the idea—but he put it on the map. He treated it like a spiritual law. Want to get rich? Start by commanding your subconscious like a general, not asking it like a beggar. Say it. Repeat it. Burn it in. Until your thoughts become orders and your body obeys.

Sound mystical?

It is.

But Hill didn't see that as a weakness—he saw it as the gateway. And that's where we start walking into stranger territory. The ether.

Now, in the early 20th century, the word "ether" was still being tossed around by scientists trying to explain how light or energy moved through space. Eventually, it was dismissed in physics. But Hill grabbed the term and ran with it.

To Hill, the ether was the medium through which thoughts traveled. A kind of invisible highway connecting all minds, all ideas, all intentions. He believed that when a thought was emotionally charged and deliberately focused, it radiated out into this ether—and through this metaphysical signal, like attracted like.

That's the root of the Law of Attraction, decades before The Secret put glitter on it.

Hill believed that thinking was a creative act, not just a mental one. That when you thought with purpose and feeling, you sent out a signal. And that signal would start pulling back opportunities, people, resources—circumstances that matched your dominant mental state.

If you were tuned to failure, failure showed up. If you tuned to abundance, abundance started orbiting. Not immediately. Not magically. But inevitably. Hill believed the universe didn't respond to words—it responded to vibration.

And the most intense example of this?

The Invisible Counselors.

This wasn't a metaphor. Hill described, in his own words, a nightly ritual in which he would summon an imaginary cabinet of advisors to guide him. They included Abraham Lincoln, Thomas Edison, Henry

Ford, Darwin, Napoleon Bonaparte, and others. Hill didn't just imagine conversations. He said the personalities began to take on lives of their own. He described dreams, voices, mental nudges—guidance that he claimed came from somewhere beyond his own brain.

Even Hill admitted it freaked him out. At one point, he stopped the exercise because he feared he was losing his grip on reality. But eventually, he came back to it—more convinced than ever that there was something real behind the experience.

This is where the modern reader either leans in or checks out.

Some will call it delusion. Hallucination. A man talking to ghosts in his sleep. Others will recognize it as visionary practice—the ability to tap into archetypes, channel insight, and communicate with the subconscious mind through symbols and imagination.

Whatever you call it, Hill made no apologies. He insisted that the real breakthroughs—the deep insights, the decisions that changed everything—came from that space. The ether. The unseen.

He didn't care if the suits thought it was unscientific. He was out to win. And if tuning into the ether gave him answers? He was going to listen.

And that's the beauty—and the terror—of Hill's mind.

He wasn't just a materialist. He wasn't just a mystic. He was both. He built his philosophy at the collision point between industrial capitalism and cosmic intuition. He spoke to the boardroom and the astral plane.

He gave you a plan, a schedule, a list.

And then he told you to talk to dead presidents in your sleep.

That's not contradiction. That's completeness.

Because the truth is—success isn't just numbers. It's energy. It's alignment. It's a war between your conscious goals and your unconscious identity. And Hill knew that most people fail not because they lack effort—but because they never learned how to change the signal they're sending into the world.

So call it mysticism. Call it madness. Call it magic.

Hill called it reality.

And if it worked for him—and for millions of readers since—maybe it's worth tuning in before you tune it out.

17

Conversations with "Invisible Counselors"

If Think and Grow Rich was Napoleon Hill's war manual for the mind, then the "Invisible Counselors" was his classified file. Buried deep in the book—almost like a dare—you'll find it. One of the strangest, most personal, most controversial revelations Hill ever made.

He wasn't alone.

At least, not in his own mind.

Hill described a practice he used almost nightly—a ritual where he summoned a mental cabinet of legendary figures to advise him. Not metaphorically. Not hypothetically. In his own words, these were vivid, interactive, even autonomous presences. People who spoke to him in dreams. Figures who offered solutions. Counselors who evolved over time, developed personalities, and started saying things Hill himself didn't consciously think.

Let that sink in.

Hill—a man considered by millions to be the godfather of rational success philosophy—was channeling imaginary friends and treating it like a boardroom strategy meeting. And he didn't try to hide it. He wrote about it in detail.

His cabinet included:

Abraham Lincoln – the moral compass

Napoleon Bonaparte – strategic brilliance

Thomas Edison – creative genius

Henry Ford – business acumen

Andrew Carnegie – wealth and influence

Charles Darwin – logical evolution

Christopher Columbus – courage and risk

Emerson – wisdom

Elbert Hubbard, Luther Burbank, and others

Each figure, Hill claimed, had unique input. He didn't just ask them questions. He observed their behaviors. He reported that they offered counsel in real-time—sometimes contradicting him, sometimes warning him, often inspiring breakthroughs.

Now, stop and think about this: this wasn't a New Age mystic sitting in a crystal dome. This was a former journalist, a capitalist philosopher, and a self-described "student of achievement" claiming he held nightly meetings with dead men. And yet—he wasn't laughed off the stage.

Why?

Because the results spoke louder than the method.

Hill was ahead of his time. What he was doing wasn't nonsense—it was mental modeling. What we now call visualization, role-playing, psychological projection—Hill was doing it before anyone had the words for it. He built avatars of excellence. He programmed his mind with the traits of the greatest men he could imagine and let them live in him.

In today's terms, we'd call this internalized archetype activation. Back then? It was called madness by some—and genius by the few who understood what was really going on.

Hill even admitted that at one point, the exercise became so real it scared him. He wrote that the personalities began to take initiative. They started showing up uninvited. Offering insight before he even asked. At that point, Hill said he backed off—temporarily. The experience had gone from empowering to... unsettling.

But that's the cost of drilling deep into the subconscious.

And that's what Hill was doing. He wasn't just using imagination to feel good—he was weaponizing it. He was installing beliefs, behaviors, confidence, and creativity by force. And his method was simple:

Choose the people whose traits you want to emulate.

Study them obsessively.

Visualize them nightly. Place them at a table in your mind.

Engage. Ask. Listen. Learn.

Let the internalized versions of those minds start shaping your decisions.

To skeptics, it was lunacy. To visionaries, it was a formula. And if you've ever had a conversation in your head with your "higher self," your future self, or a mentor's voice—congratulations. You've done the same thing.

Hill just did it with more intensity—and less apology.

What this really shows is the core of Hill's genius: he believed the mind was programmable to an extreme degree. And he wasn't interested in minor updates. He wanted full-blown psychological reinstallation. His invisible counselors were a delivery system for new identity.

Want to think like Lincoln? Sit across from him every night for six months and start absorbing how he responds to your problems. Want Edison's creative genius? Ask him what he'd do with your business. Want Ford's indifference to critics? Watch him laugh at your fears.

Hill was building a new self, piece by piece, from the inside out.

That's not delusion.

That's intentional evolution.

And maybe the most terrifying part? It works. When you install new reference points—when you let stronger, more decisive, more powerful voices occupy your mental space—you change. Your instincts shift. Your default reactions get upgraded. Your old identity starts losing power.

That's why Hill didn't care if you thought he was crazy. He was winning the internal war. And to him, that was all that mattered.

So what are the invisible counselors, really?

They're not ghosts. They're not hallucinations.

They're the refusal to be limited by the current contents of your character.

They're a blueprint for borrowing strength until you've built your own.

And in a world addicted to imitation and paralyzed by indecision, Hill's message still stands:

You don't have to figure it all out alone. Build the table. Fill the chairs. And start asking better minds for better answers—even if those minds exist only in the one place that truly matters: your own.

18

The Blurred Line Between Inspiration and Delusion

Napoleon Hill walked a tightrope most men are too terrified to even approach—the razor-thin line between inspiration and delusion. And he didn't just walk it. He danced on it. He stared into the void, saw what could be, and dared to call it real before anyone else believed it. That's the core of his genius—and the root of every accusation against him.

Because when you live like that—speaking your vision out loud before it exists—people either call you a prophet... or a fraud.

Sometimes they're both right.

Let's be blunt. Hill made outrageous claims. Conversations with industrial titans with no paper trail. A twenty-year mission from Andrew Carnegie with no evidence. Hearing advice from dead men in his nightly rituals. Believing his deaf son would hear again through sheer force of thought. Writing about ether and invisible energy fields decades before new-age bookstores existed.

Sounds crazy, right?

But now look around.

The same world that mocked Hill is now obsessed with "manifestation," "neuroplasticity," "vibrational alignment," and "quantum consciousness." The exact same people who'd laugh at Hill's ether now build careers selling it under new packaging. The difference? Hill didn't soften the edges. He didn't put it in a TED Talk. He lived it, raw and unfiltered.

And that's what made him dangerous.

Inspiration is socially acceptable. Delusion is not. But the line between the two isn't moral—it's results. If your belief pays off, you're a visionary. If it doesn't, you're insane. The world worships winners and pathologizes the ones who fall short.

But Hill didn't care. He knew the game.

He wrote his life into existence—even when the facts didn't always back him up. That's not lying. That's vision under construction. That's belief in its rawest form.

He saw the world as it could be and treated it like it already was. And that freaks people out. Because most of society is built on the opposite principle—wait until it's real, then believe it. Hill said, believe it until it becomes real. That's not delusion. That's the cost of creation.

But let's not sugarcoat it—Hill wasn't infallible. He made mistakes. He failed repeatedly. He overpromised. He inflated his resume. He edited reality to fit his message. That's not ideal—but it's also not unique. Every great builder breaks a few rules while figuring out what works.

So the question isn't, Was Hill always accurate?

The question is, Was Hill's vision worth the distortion?

And the answer is obvious. His work has helped millions of people escape mental prisons. It's sparked empires. Rewritten personal narratives. Fueled turnarounds, breakthroughs, and awakenings. That kind of impact doesn't come from neatness. It comes from someone willing to go further than what's reasonable.

That's where the line blurs.

Because delusion, at its root, is belief that offends the current consensus. Hill's entire worldview offended consensus reality. He told people that their thoughts created their future—that reality was clay in the hands of the focused mind. He said fear was a habit. Poverty a mindset. Success a decision.

To the masses? That sounded insane.

But that's what makes it powerful.

You don't need inspiration when everything's working. You need it when you're on your knees, broke, humiliated, doubting every breath—and still trying to light a fire in your chest. That's where Hill lived. Not in boardrooms. In the trenches. And if he had to lie a little to get himself out? To get you out?

So be it.

Because here's the paradox most people can't handle: sometimes delusion is the only way forward. You have to believe in a version of yourself that doesn't yet exist. You have to speak truths that haven't manifested yet. You have to become insane to break out of the collective hypnosis of safety, fear, and mediocrity.

Hill understood this.

And if that makes him dangerous—good.

Because the world doesn't need more careful thinkers. It needs firestarters—people willing to push so hard against their own limits that the line between what's real and what's imagined disappears. People who live so deep in their vision that they drag reality forward with them.

Inspiration and delusion share a spine. The difference is whether you quit before the outcome catches up.

Hill never quit.

That's why he's still here.

That's why his words still haunt the shelves.

And that's why, if you've got the guts to dream so loud people call you delusional—you might just be walking the exact same path he paved.

19

Failed Ventures, Broken Promises, and Worse

You don't get to write the most influential self-help book in history without dragging a few skeletons behind you. And Napoleon Hill? He had a graveyard.

The man who taught millions how to succeed spent much of his own life circling the edge of failure. Not quiet, humble failure—but public, catastrophic, lawsuit-drenched, reputation-wrecking failure. Failed ventures. Unpaid debts. Promises made and abandoned. Business partners burned. And yeah, criminal accusations too.

This isn't the cleaned-up Napoleon Hill of the Foundation brochures. This is Hill as he really lived—on the edge, always one deal away from greatness, always one disaster away from vanishing. And somehow, always talking his way back into the game.

Let's not pretend this was a series of flukes. This was a pattern. A cycle. Hill would have an idea—bold, ambitious, wrapped in gold. He'd sell it. Hard. Investors would line up. Plans would be made. Marketing would start. And then—collapse. Either the money dried up, the logistics fell apart, or Hill himself bailed before the dust settled. Sometimes all three.

Take Hill's Golden Rule Magazine. Launched in 1919, it was supposed to be the flagship of his growing success empire. A moral, spiritual, business-focused publication meant to elevate the American worker. Hill marketed it with righteous fire—and convinced investors it would change the world.

Two years later, it folded.

Litigation followed. Hill was accused of inflating circulation numbers, failing to pay staff, and misleading backers. Nothing stuck legally, but the damage was done. That was the first major hit to his reputation—and it wouldn't be the last.

In the 1920s and early '30s, Hill launched a string of business schools and "Success Colleges" based on his philosophy. He claimed he could train anyone to be a titan of industry—provided they followed his 13 principles. It sounded great. And for a while, it worked. People signed up. Money came in.

And then—just like clockwork—things fell apart.

Students complained. Vendors went unpaid. One school in Chicago barely lasted a year before shuttering with no explanation. In multiple cities, Hill left behind debts, unpaid rent, and silence. He became known not just for his writing—but for running when things got hot.

And then there were the accusations.

In 1923, Hill filed for bankruptcy. His finances were a mess. Creditors were circling. He claimed, as always, that the fault lay with external forces—economic downturns, dishonest partners, spiritual interference. But others weren't so forgiving. They said Hill had overpromised, lied about earnings, and walked away from obligations.

Throughout his life, various lawsuits and accusations followed him. Fraud. Misrepresentation. Breach of contract. Many didn't go to trial. Others were quietly settled. In one instance, he was reportedly arrested for violating business laws in Florida—but vanished before prosecution. Whether that was self-preservation or something more calculated depends on who you ask.

Hill's defenders say he was misunderstood. A visionary ahead of his time. A man who couldn't be bothered with paperwork and logistics because he was too busy thinking rich. They say he was preyed upon by schemers and saboteurs. Maybe.

His critics say he was a scam artist with a gift for marketing and no intention of delivering. A man who sold hope like snake oil. A guy who used words like "faith" and "autosuggestion" to dodge accountability and escape judgment. They might not be wrong either.

Here's the real truth, uncomfortable as it is: Hill was both.

He was a genius and a liability. A prophet of possibility and a walking PR disaster. He burned bridges and built kingdoms—sometimes on the same day. His failures weren't tragic. They were epic. His betrayals weren't petty—they were structural. But through it all, one thing stayed consistent:

He never stopped believing in the message.

Even when his ventures failed. Even when his friends turned. Even when creditors came knocking. Hill kept writing. Kept speaking. Kept selling the idea that you are the architect of your life.

And here's the wild part—it worked.

Because his personal chaos never erased the power of the system he taught. The 13 principles still work. They've helped millions, built empires, transformed entire industries. So how do you reconcile that?

You don't.

You hold both truths at once.

Napoleon Hill was not a saint. He was not a straight shooter. But he was also not a con man in the traditional sense. He believed every word he wrote. His system wasn't a scam. It was real. He just couldn't always live up to it himself. And that's not fraud—that's human nature under pressure.

So yes—his ventures failed.

Yes—he broke promises.

Yes—he was accused, sued, chased, and run out of town more than once.

But he also left behind one of the most powerful frameworks for self-mastery ever put to paper.

And that contradiction?

That's the price of genius.

20

Lawsuits and Disillusioned Followers

For every copy of Think and Grow Rich that changed a life, there's a paper trail behind it full of lawsuits, failed enterprises, and former believers turned bitter. Napoleon Hill wasn't just surrounded by admirers. He left behind a long line of disillusioned followers—people who invested in his vision, bought into the man, and watched it all fall apart.

And no one wants to talk about that.

The Napoleon Hill Foundation won't put it on the brochure. Motivational speakers quoting Hill on stage won't mention it. But it's there. In court filings. In unpaid invoices. In testimonials from people who trusted him with their time, money, and hope—only to end up with nothing but a story of what could have been.

This isn't fiction. It's part of the legacy. And if you're going to understand Hill, you can't just read the success stories. You have to dig into the aftermath.

The Pattern of Lawsuits

Hill's history with litigation wasn't incidental—it was habitual. From the 1910s through the 1940s, he was sued repeatedly by former business partners, creditors, employees, and clients. The accusations were usually the same: misrepresentation, unpaid debts, and breach of contract.

In the 1920s, one of his business schools shut down suddenly, leaving students with no refunds and no explanations. Some filed complaints. Others filed lawsuits. But by the time the legal dust kicked up,

Hill was gone—moved to another city, starting over under a new banner with the same core pitch: follow me, and I'll teach you how to win.

In one high-profile case, Hill was accused of using fraudulent promotional materials to solicit investment for one of his early "Success Colleges." He promised national expansion. Big returns. Guaranteed personal growth. It was all marketing. There was no solid plan, no sustainable infrastructure. Just Hill, his charisma, and a stack of dreams.

When it all crumbled, lawsuits followed.

And yet—he walked away. Rebranded. Restarted. Reframed the collapse as "lessons learned." That was Hill's genius and his curse: he could survive anything because he never stopped talking like he'd already won.

The Followers Who Believed—and Got Burned

It wasn't just investors and creditors who walked away feeling duped. It was ordinary people. Teachers. Clerks. Salesmen. People who read The Law of Success or Hill's magazine and thought, finally—someone who understands how I think. They didn't just buy into the product. They bought into him.

Many signed up for courses, seminars, and special access to Hill's programs. He offered direct mentorship at times—promising personal transformation, tailored business advice, even one-on-one coaching. Some paid significant sums to be "in the circle." And then?

Nothing.

Or worse—half-delivered products, broken promises, and silence.

One man from Chicago reportedly invested his life savings into opening a Hill-branded success school—on Hill's word alone. When the money dried up, Hill disappeared from communication. The man sued. He lost. Hill was untouchable by then—legally shielded or just skilled at vanishing before the court date.

These weren't outliers. They were casualties of a man who believed so deeply in his own system that he often failed to deliver it responsibly.

Vision or Vanity?

Hill never saw himself as a scam artist. That's the hardest part to reconcile. He genuinely believed he was doing good. He saw setbacks as tests, failures as proof of resistance, and criticism as evidence that he was challenging the status quo.

But the people who followed him? They weren't looking for mythology. They wanted results.

Some got them. Many didn't. And when the system didn't work—when autosuggestion didn't pay the bills, when faith didn't fix the family, when organized planning didn't stop the bank from foreclosing—they didn't blame themselves.

They blamed him.

The result was a shadow movement of disillusioned followers. Quiet. Embarrassed. Angry. Not loud enough to make headlines, but present. And painfully aware that the man who preached success wasn't always living it—or sharing it.

What Hill Owed—and What He Didn't

Did Hill owe his followers perfection? No. Did he owe them honesty? Yes. And that's where things got murky.

Hill's confidence often slipped into overpromising. His ambition outpaced his infrastructure. He could sell a vision so powerful it felt like a contract—and then vanish when reality failed to keep up. That's not just marketing. That's ethical negligence.

But at the same time, Hill never forced anyone to follow him. He didn't con people in the dark. He sold possibility. And possibility is addictive.

So who's to blame?

The man who sold the dream—or the people who forgot that dreams still require discipline?

The truth lives in the middle. Hill was both an architect of empowerment and a repeat offender in the court of accountability. He changed lives. He also cost people their time, money, and trust.

And that duality? It's not a flaw in his legacy—it is his legacy.

Because greatness doesn't come in clean lines.

And the closer you fly to the sun, the more people you burn along the way.

21

The Split Between Teachings and Personal Life

There's a line that runs through the life of Napoleon Hill like a fault under pressure. On one side, the teachings: crystal-clear principles, obsessive discipline, relentless faith. On the other side, the man: inconsistent, chaotic, debt-ridden, full of broken promises and reinventions. And between them? A chasm most of his followers never dared to look into.

But if you really want to understand Hill—not worship him, not bury him, but understand him—you have to walk right up to that line and stare down into the contradiction.

Because the man who wrote the manual for success didn't always follow it. And that's not just a footnote. That's the story.

A Life Built on Principles He Couldn't Always Live By
Hill gave the world thirteen principles to think, act, and grow rich. But if you stacked those principles next to his personal timeline—his bankruptcies, his vanishing acts, his lawsuits, his imploding ventures—you'd swear he hadn't read his own book.

Faith? The man lived in fear of being exposed more than once.

Persistence? Yes—but often applied to starting over after abandoning something else.

Organized planning? His ventures folded like paper hats.

Definiteness of purpose? Sure—until the next city, the next investor, the next relaunch.

That's the paradox. His teachings were clean. His life was messy. And yet, millions have used those teachings to build fortunes, break addictions, reinvent themselves. That kind of impact doesn't come from a con artist. It comes from a flawed transmitter of truth.

Hill didn't invent the principles of success. He channeled them. And like all imperfect vessels, he leaked along the way.

Preacher of Success, Practitioner of Chaos

It's easy to follow a clean example. It's harder to extract value from a contradiction. But that's what Hill demands. Because here was a man who could teach prosperity while living in poverty. Who could write about faith while drowning in lawsuits. Who could tell others how to take control of their destiny while spending his own life dodging creditors, collapsing businesses, and fractured relationships.

But what if that's the point?

What if Hill's life was the laboratory—and we were never supposed to copy his biography, but extract the method from the mess?

Hill was a preacher of personal power who often lived like a man under siege. He spoke with the clarity of a prophet but lived with the instability of a gambler. That's not fraud. That's the tension between vision and reality. Between the world as it is and the world as it could be.

He taught better than he lived. That's the truth.

But in a culture full of liars who live better than they teach, I'll take the guy who tried.

The Public Image vs. The Private Man

Publicly, Hill was confidence incarnate. Sharp suits. Commanding tone. Authoritative presence. He didn't sell advice—he sold certainty. He spoke like a man who had cracked the code and was now kind enough to let the rest of us in on it.

Privately? He was often broke. On the run. Dependent on the next gig, the next publication deal, the next investor who believed the pitch. He had a volatile marriage. He moved constantly. He burned through trust as quickly as he built it.

And still—he believed.

That's what sets Hill apart. Most people collapse under the weight of hypocrisy. Hill leaned into it. He kept teaching what he knew was true, even when he failed to live it out. That's a different kind of integrity—the kind most people don't understand. Because we're trained to believe that only the flawless have wisdom.

But history says otherwise.

Many of the most transformative thinkers were personal disasters. Carl Jung cheated on his wife and rewrote the subconscious. Hemingway drank himself blind and gave us truth. Martin Luther had breakdowns and rewrote Christianity. And Hill—Hill stumbled his way through bankruptcy court while giving the world a roadmap to freedom.

That's not failure.

That's humanity under pressure.

What Do You Do with the Contradiction?

You don't excuse it.

You use it.

You recognize that the value of a message isn't invalidated by the weakness of the messenger. That wisdom can come from a broken voice. That truth is still truth, even if the man delivering it can't always live it.

Hill's teachings are clean because they had to be. His life was chaos. The philosophy was his anchor. His lifeline. And even when he was failing it, he never stopped refining it.

So don't worship Hill. And don't crucify him either.

Learn from both.

From the man who knew the way, and from the man who sometimes got lost on it.

Because if Napoleon Hill taught us anything, it's that your past doesn't disqualify your future. Your mess doesn't cancel your message. And your struggle to live by the truth doesn't mean it's not true.

He was flawed.

So are you.

Apply the principles anyway.

And keep moving.

22

Outwitting the Devil – The Lost Confession

The Suppressed Manuscript and Its Eventual Release
Outwitting the Devil isn't just another Napoleon Hill book—it's a bomb that sat under the floorboards for 73 years, with the pin still in. A confession. A warning. A psychic revolt against everything Hill had spent decades polishing. It was never meant to be read by the public—at least, not while Hill was alive. And maybe not even while America still thought it believed in freedom.

Because in Outwitting the Devil, Hill doesn't just share ideas. He spills blood.

He breaks the facade. Steps out of the polished author suit. And sits down with the one voice no motivational thinker ever wants to admit they hear—the voice of doubt. Of fear. Of stagnation. Hill names that voice for what it is: The Devil. Not with horns and flames, but with a chilling intellect and calm voice that explains, in surgical detail, how most people are controlled without ever realizing it.

That manuscript? Hill finished it in 1938.

Then he buried it.

Why It Was Buried
Hill's wife, Annie Lou, wouldn't let it be published. She feared the backlash. And she was right.

The book calls out the church. The school system. The government. It dismantles conventional morality and points the finger at the institutions people are trained to trust. It presents a Devil who isn't scary because he's evil—but because he's efficient. Because he doesn't need to torment people in hell when he can distract them on Earth.

Hill had already spent years trying to get people to understand the power of the mind. But this book? It was too raw. Too revealing. It showed the war inside the man behind Think and Grow Rich. And it showed just how hard he had to fight to apply the very principles he preached.

The message wasn't marketable. It wasn't polished. It was radioactive.

And so, like most truths in a polite society, it got locked away.

The Manuscript Survives

Hill died in 1970. The manuscript sat in a vault at the Napoleon Hill Foundation for decades—known only to a few insiders. Occasionally referenced. Never released.

It wasn't until 2011—over seventy years after Hill wrote it—that the book finally hit shelves.

Think about that.

Hill wrote this in the shadow of the Great Depression, when fascism was rising and institutions were cracking. It read like prophecy then. It reads like diagnosis now.

When it was finally released, it wasn't welcomed with parades. It was met with confusion, resistance—and for those paying attention—reverence. Because this wasn't Hill the legend. This was Hill the man, stripped of the performance, staring into the dark mirror of human nature and reporting back what he saw.

The Confession: Drift, Fear, and the Real Enemy

The Devil in the book doesn't scream. He speaks like a bureaucrat. Calm. Rational. And absolutely in control.

He says he owns the minds of 98% of humanity. Not through violence. Through drift—that state of mental sleepwalking where people stop thinking, stop questioning, and just go along with the path of least resistance. School trains it into you. Religion locks it in. Fear polices the rest.

And Hill? He admits—he almost got taken by it himself.

The book isn't just an interview with darkness. It's a map of how Hill nearly lost the war inside his own mind. He describes failure, shame, confusion, and the creeping paralysis that kept him stuck despite knowing all the right principles. It's a self-help author standing naked before the void and asking, Why isn't this working?

And the Devil answers.

Not with fire—but with facts. You failed because you doubted. You drifted. You let fear whisper instead of faith command. You outsourced your decisions. You thought you had time.

Hill doesn't deny it.

He confesses.

That's what makes the book so important—not as a motivational tool, but as a spiritual X-ray. It shows what the polished books don't: that the war for your life is mental. And that knowing the rules doesn't mean you're immune to the pull of drift.

The Impact of the Release

When Outwitting the Devil was finally released, it was too late to cancel Hill—but not too late to wake people up. The book instantly split the room.

Some called it weird. Off-brand. Too dark. Too religious. Others said it was the most important thing Hill ever wrote.

Because here's the truth: Think and Grow Rich was a weapon.

Outwitting the Devil was the warning label.

It was the missing half of the system. The part where Hill admits that mindset isn't enough unless you guard it ruthlessly. That desire alone doesn't save you from fear. That you can know the way out—and still sit in the cell.

He also showed us that freedom isn't something you earn once. It's a decision you make daily. Or the Devil takes back the wheel.

Hill's own life, with all its contradictions, failures, and reinventions, only makes this book hit harder. He wasn't immune. He was a case study.

And in finally publishing this lost confession, Hill gave the world something far more valuable than more feel-good quotes.

He gave us proof that the real enemy is not poverty, or failure, or bad luck.

It's the slow, invisible decay of your own mind.

And if you don't outwit it—something else will.

23

Harsh Critique of Religion, Education, and Fear

Napoleon Hill didn't just flirt with controversy—he lit a cigar and walked straight into it. In Outwitting the Devil, he ripped the mask off the pillars of polite society and said what few men of his time (or ours) have the spine to admit: the institutions we trust the most are often the ones that make us weak, obedient, and afraid.

Hill didn't whisper it.

He declared it.

In plain language, he accused organized religion, formal education, and fear-based parenting of being the primary delivery systems for mental slavery. Not in some metaphorical way. In a literal, mechanical sense. They trained people to drift—Hill's term for the slow, zombie-like surrender of free will. And drifting, he said, is how the Devil gains control.

Religion: Weaponized Guilt, Programmed Fear

Hill didn't trash spirituality. He made that distinction clear. In fact, he believed in what he called Infinite Intelligence—a higher order of consciousness, accessible through faith, meditation, and personal alignment. But organized religion? That's where he brought out the knife.

According to Hill, religion trains people what to think, not how to think. It teaches submission over sovereignty. Blind belief over critical inquiry. And worst of all, it uses fear as its primary motivator.

Fear of hell.

Fear of sin.

Fear of punishment.

Fear of divine judgment.

Not love. Not truth. Fear.

Hill saw this as spiritual blackmail. He said when a child is taught to fear God instead of understand God, the game is already lost. Their subconscious is programmed for guilt. For self-sabotage. For a lifetime of running from damnation instead of running toward creation.

And that guilt doesn't just sit in church pews. It leaks into every other part of life—relationships, ambition, sexuality, self-worth. It creates adults who second-guess their power because they were told as children that power was dangerous.

Hill's solution? Dismantle the fear. Keep the faith. Throw out the dogma.

Education: The Factory of Mental Drift

If religion was Hill's first target, education was the second—and he hit it even harder.

He said the school system wasn't designed to build thinkers. It was built to produce compliant workers. And he was right. Still is. The average school doesn't teach students to think critically, question authority, or build wealth. It teaches memorization, obedience, and dependency.

Hill said schools teach "facts, not truth."

They reward recitation, not imagination.

They prepare you to pass tests, not to pass through life as a sovereign human being.

By the time a student finishes school, Hill argued, they've already been trained to drift—to follow schedules, accept grades as identity, and outsource their purpose to institutions. They've learned to sit still, shut up, raise their hand, and ask permission for everything. Sound familiar?

Hill's prescription wasn't subtle: burn the blueprint. Start teaching children the principles of definiteness of purpose, self-discipline, creative imagination, and spiritual agency. But society doesn't want children like that. It wants taxpayers. Consumers. Obedient gear-turners.

He saw it. He called it. And he was ignored.

Because what Hill described was the enemy of empire: a free thinker.

Fear: The Universal Control Mechanism

At the center of all of Hill's critiques—religion, school, family, government—is the same virus:

Fear.

Hill doesn't dance around this. He goes surgical. In Outwitting the Devil, he breaks down fear into its primary forms:

Fear of poverty

Fear of criticism

Fear of ill health

Fear of loss of love

Fear of old age

Fear of death

These six fears, he said, are installed early, reinforced constantly, and used to manipulate people into surrendering their will.

It's not a conspiracy theory.

It's how the system works.

And Hill doesn't blame shadowy elites. He blames you—for allowing it. For entertaining fear. For feeding it with indecision, with procrastination, with compromise. He says fear can't control you unless you give it room to operate.

The Devil in Hill's book even admits: "I control people by getting them to submit to fear." That's it. That's the playbook. Install fear. Trigger it at will. Reap the benefits of a distracted, dependent population.

You see it in media. In medicine. In politics. But Hill said the real battlefield is your mind. And if you don't fight back there, it doesn't matter what external freedoms you think you have.

You're already captured.

The Common Thread: The Death of Personal Authority

When Hill attacked religion and education, he wasn't just criticizing bad teaching. He was targeting the slow erosion of personal authority. The stripping away of your inner compass. The theft of your ability to say, "I decide what's true."

That's what Think and Grow Rich tried to restore.

That's what Outwitting the Devil exposed.

And that's why Hill is still so dangerous today.

Because once you realize fear is a product, religion is a leash, and school is a factory, you stop being manageable. You stop being predictable. You stop being a customer, a voter, a patient—and start being a creator.

Hill wasn't trying to burn down the world.

He was trying to reboot it.

From the inside out.

So yes—he criticized religion.

Yes—he called out the schools.

And yes—he declared war on fear.

Because he knew what most people don't:

You can't think and grow rich if you're still scared and staying small.

24

Was This His Most Honest Work?

Yes. Outwitting the Devil was Napoleon Hill's most honest work. And that's exactly why it stayed buried for seventy-three years.

Because honesty isn't clean. It doesn't fit the brand. It doesn't sell at seminars or sit nicely on a self-help shelf next to smiling gurus promising six figures in six weeks. Honesty is raw. It's dark. It's uncomfortable. And Outwitting the Devil was all of that—Napoleon Hill without the polish, without the pitch, without the salesman's grin.

This wasn't Hill the prophet of prosperity. This was Hill the man—battered, unsure, and staring straight into the abyss of his own mind.

And for the first time, he didn't flinch.

A Window into the Man, Not the Myth

Most people know Hill through Think and Grow Rich, the polished product. The system. The blueprint. It's structured, carefully composed, and delivered like divine truth. But Outwitting the Devil is what happens when that same man realizes that even the blueprint has blind spots.

In Think and Grow Rich, Hill was the teacher.

In Outwitting the Devil, he's the student again.

He admits his doubts. He admits his fears. He admits that even with all his principles, all his knowledge, all his preaching—he still found himself stuck. Paralyzed. Lost. Not forever. But long enough to realize that the biggest enemy wasn't external.

It was within.

That kind of confession? It doesn't come from a man trying to impress you. It comes from a man trying to free you.

He Turned the Spotlight on the System—and on Himself

Hill didn't stop at criticizing institutions. He turned the blade inward. He wrote about how he'd been seduced by comfort. How his success almost made him soft. How drift—his word for unconscious living—was something he had personally tasted.

This wasn't theoretical.

It was autobiographical.

He spoke about failure with clarity. Not the kind of failure that fuels a comeback story, but the kind that threatens your very identity. He didn't say, "I stumbled and got back up." He said, "I was on the verge of becoming a permanent drifter."

He spoke about fear—how it crept in through parenting, religion, education. But he also admitted he let it in. That he fed it with self-doubt. That he gave it power by playing small, even while writing big.

This wasn't for show.

This was a man telling the truth while it was still dangerous to do so.

The Devil Wasn't a Gimmick—It Was His Shadow

Some people read the book and think, "The Devil? Really?" Like it's some theatrical device.

It wasn't.

The Devil was Hill's shadow. His unspoken fears, his internal saboteur, his lower self given a voice. Carl Jung would've nodded in understanding. Hill gave the darkness a name so he could interrogate it.

He didn't avoid it. He argued with it.

And he let it win round after round.

Until he realized the Devil's entire strategy came down to this: drift.

Not sin. Not evil. Just numbness. Mindlessness. The slow erosion of personal power. And Hill admitted—this is how the Devil nearly got him. Not through scandal. Through stagnation.

If that's not honesty, what is?

Buried Because It Cut Too Close to the Bone

So why didn't he publish it?

Because this book would've ruined him in his time.

It questioned organized religion at a time when church and reputation were inseparable. It accused schools of producing factory workers instead of free thinkers. It told people that their parents might've been their first jailers. It named fear as the state's favorite tool.

Hill's wife knew what this book would do.

It wasn't just a career risk—it was social suicide.

But maybe Hill knew that too.

Maybe he wrote it not for 1938, but for a future generation that could handle the truth. Not just the success formulas, but the internal war. Not just the steps, but the sabotage. Not just the light—but the darkness you have to pass through to earn it.

The Truth Behind the Curtain

Yes—Outwitting the Devil was Hill's most honest work.

Because it stripped away the final illusion: that success is clean.

It's not.

It's bloody. It's confusing. It demands clarity in the face of chaos. And sometimes, it demands that you sit across from the darkest part of yourself and listen.

That's what Hill did.

Not because it was marketable.

Because it was necessary.

And now, all these years later, that honesty is still doing what it was always meant to do—not to make you feel good, but to wake you up.

Not just to your potential.

But to the war going on inside you right now.

25

How His Legacy Was Curated
and Commodified

Napoleon Hill's legacy didn't just survive—it was sanitized. Cleaned up. Packaged. Stripped of contradiction and rebranded for mass consumption. The man who spent decades battling failure, scandal, and self-doubt was polished into a success saint. The grit was buried. The lawsuits were forgotten. The Devil was gagged.

In his place, we got the statue.

The curriculum.

The seminars.

The Foundation.

The corporate endorsements.

And in doing so, we didn't just preserve Hill's message—we weaponized it for the marketplace.

Hill's philosophy became a brand. And once something becomes a brand, it stops being dangerous. It stops being human. It becomes product. And that's exactly what happened.

From Revolutionary to Mascot

Make no mistake—Hill wasn't writing for the elite. He wasn't a university intellectual. He was a backwoods kid from Virginia who taught himself to think like a king. His words weren't academic. They were urgent. They were written for the hungry, the cornered, the fired, the broke, the broken.

But after he died?

The Napoleon Hill Foundation emerged like a PR firm with a time machine.

Suddenly, Hill's mess was a footnote. The foundation reissued his work, repackaged his image, and began distributing his ideas with a layer of Teflon optimism. The chaos? Gone. The controversy? Ignored. The Devil? Quietly locked back in the vault for another half-century.

In its place: platitudes. "Whatever the mind can conceive and believe..." you know the rest. Hill's face became a meme. His quotes became PowerPoint slides. His once-electric ideas were reduced to corporate training fodder and bumper stickers.

It worked. It sells. But don't confuse the merchandise for the man.

Self-Help as Industry, Not Philosophy

Hill wasn't trying to start a self-help industry. He was trying to spark a psychological rebellion. But once the movement caught fire, it didn't take long for someone to show up with a bucket—and a sales funnel.

Hill's system got sliced into coaching programs, DVD sets, certification courses, masterminds, branded journals, online challenges, "Hill Method" success summits. His teachings were extracted and mass-produced for maximum monetization.

You want access to success? Buy the bundle.

You want inner power? Click subscribe.

And all of it wrapped in Hill's image—as if the man who couldn't hold a business together for more than two years would be smiling at a Shopify checkout page.

The self-help industry didn't just adopt Hill. It consumed him. Because he was the original blueprint. The model. The first to say: your thoughts shape your reality. Everyone else just added better lighting and more upsells.

But here's the punchline: Hill never cashed in. Not like the empire built off his bones. His estate didn't reap the rewards that now flow through speaking circuits and leadership brands.

The man who gave the world the key to the vault?

Died without holding the deed.

The Sanitization of Danger

The most damning part of Hill's legacy isn't that it was commodified. It's that it was sanitized. The sharp edges were filed down. The weirdness was removed. The Devil was locked away.

Because it's hard to sell Hill's real story.

It's not convenient to talk about the lawsuits. The failed ventures. The bad business deals. The multiple bankruptcies. The accusations of fraud. The angry former students. The disillusioned partners. The psychological collapse. The inner war.

It's much easier to say:

"Napoleon Hill was a wise old man who discovered the secret to success, lived happily ever after, and now you can too—for just $997."

Bullshit.

Hill battled for every insight he ever taught.

He failed at living up to his own principles. Repeatedly.

But he kept showing up.

That's what made him great.

And that's what's been lost.

Because Hill's legacy, as curated today, is designed to be consumable. Risk-free. Comfortable. It's success without struggle. Growth without pain. Transformation without accountability.

In other words—exactly the kind of thing the real Hill would have destroyed with a single sentence.

Reclaiming the Man from the Monument

If we want to understand Hill, we have to steal him back from the marketing department. We have to pull him off the pedestal, sit him down, and listen to the man behind the myth.

The one who doubted.

Who drifted.

Who chased impossible dreams and failed, then dared to write a book telling you how not to.

The real Napoleon Hill wasn't clean. He wasn't safe. He wasn't a motivational bot chirping affirmations. He was a man at war with himself—and he won just enough battles to map the way out for the rest of us.

That's the legacy that matters.

Not the branding.

Not the quotes.

Not the logo.

But the fire.

The raw, contradictory, unkillable belief that no matter how many times you fall, no matter how deep the hole or how loud the doubt—

you can still choose to rise.

And if that doesn't sell as well?

Good.

That means it's finally telling the truth.

26

The Foundation's Role in Controlling the Narrative

The Napoleon Hill Foundation presents itself as the guardian of a legacy—caretakers of wisdom, preservers of truth, promoters of Hill's life-changing philosophy. And on the surface, that's exactly what they do. They publish the books. They license the quotes. They stamp Hill's face on planners, webinars, and leadership retreats.

But dig deeper, and it becomes clear: they aren't just preserving Napoleon Hill's legacy.

They're editing it.

Because if there's one thing the Foundation understands better than anyone, it's this: you can't sell contradiction. You can't market lawsuits, bankruptcy, mysticism, or spiritual warfare to the same corporate audience you're trying to convince that Hill is a clean-cut business icon.

So they did what most institutions do when the truth gets messy.

They cleaned it up.

They kept the message.

And buried the man.

The Sanitized Hill: Perfect, Predictable, Profitable

Read any modern bio of Hill published through the Foundation. You'll see the same storyline:

Humble beginnings.

Inspired by Andrew Carnegie.

Interviewed the greats.

Wrote Think and Grow Rich.

Created a timeless philosophy that changed the world.

All technically true.

All radically incomplete.

Missing

27

What Gets Left Out of the "Official" Story

The "official" story of Napoleon Hill is clean, digestible, and market-tested. A nice narrative arc: dirt-poor kid from rural Virginia receives divine inspiration from Andrew Carnegie, interviews the world's greatest minds, survives the Great Depression, writes the ultimate self-help book, and leaves behind a timeless legacy of success.

It's inspirational. It's profitable. It's also incomplete.

Because what gets left out of the "official" story is everything that makes the real story worth telling. Everything raw. Everything uncomfortable. Everything human. The mess, the mystery, the contradictions—those are the pieces that turn Hill from a brand into a man. And the Foundation, the seminar circuit, and the sanitized biographies have gone to great lengths to make sure you never see them.

Why?

Because the truth doesn't sell as well as the slogan.

The Carnegie Myth: Gospel or Marketing?

Let's start with the cornerstone: Andrew Carnegie giving Hill a secret 20-year mission to unlock the secrets of success by interviewing 500 of the most powerful men in America.

It's a great story. But there's no paper trail. No diary entries. No letters. No mention of Hill in Carnegie's surviving documents. Not a shred of contemporary evidence to prove the meeting ever took place.

And the Foundation? They repeat it anyway. Every bio, every press release, every reprint of Think and Grow Rich carries that same origin story. Not because it's verified—but because it sells.

And that tells you everything about how the story has been shaped. Not around facts.

Around function.

The Lawsuits, the Failures, the Debt
Hill's business record was, in plain terms, a train wreck.

He launched magazines, schools, and training companies that collapsed in debt and litigation. He promised investors national franchises, guaranteed returns, and revolutionary success systems—most of which vanished before they ever launched. He filed for bankruptcy multiple times. He was sued. He disappeared from towns. He reinvented himself under new company names and moved on.

That's not rumor. That's the documented pattern of his life.

Yet none of that makes it into the curated Hill curriculum. You'll never hear about the Chicago success school that collapsed after a year. Or the magazine that left creditors unpaid. Or the government complaints filed by jilted business partners.

The official version omits the financial chaos, the burned bridges, and the public failures. Because those details raise dangerous questions.

Like: If he couldn't run a business, why should I trust his advice on how to succeed?

The Foundation would rather you didn't ask.

Outwitting the Devil: The Book They Buried
The biggest omission of all?

Outwitting the Devil.

Hill wrote it in 1938, and it didn't see the light of day until 2011—seventy-three years later. Why? Because it was too honest. Too radical. Too anti-institution.

The book dismantled religion, education, politics, and parenting. It showed Hill battling fear, failure, depression, and spiritual inertia. It introduced the concept of "drift"—the passive, soul-numbing state that 98% of humanity lives in, controlled by an invisible, symbolic Devil.

The Foundation kept it sealed for decades, calling it "too controversial." What they meant was: it shattered the brand. It revealed the internal chaos Hill fought daily. It admitted that the man who wrote Think and Grow Rich nearly lost the war with his own mind.

And that's not the Hill they want you to see.

They want you to see the infallible architect of success—not the flawed philosopher who had to battle his demons just to function.

But guess what?

The flawed version is more powerful.

Because he's real.

The Mysticism, the Ether, the Ghost Cabinet

Hill didn't just write about strategy. He wrote about energy. Ether. Infinite Intelligence. He held nightly meetings in his imagination with a cabinet of dead historical figures—Lincoln, Edison, Carnegie, Bonaparte—who offered him advice and occasionally spoke back without invitation.

He believed thoughts had frequencies. That the brain could transmit and receive ideas like radio waves. That the subconscious mind, if properly tuned, could tap into universal intelligence and bend reality.

He said these things plainly. In his books. But you'll barely hear about it today.

Because in the Foundation-approved version, Hill is an early motivational speaker. A business sage. A positive-thinking capitalist.

But Hill was a mystic in a three-piece suit.

And they can't market mysticism to Fortune 500 training departments—so they just cut that part out.

The Man vs. The Monument

The real Napoleon Hill was a storm.

He failed. He lied. He disappeared. He reinvented. He believed. He suffered. He kept going.

That's the story that gets left out.

The official version needs him to be clean, linear, infallible. The truth is that he was none of those things. And that's what makes his work so damn important.

Because he wasn't a guru talking down from a mountaintop.

He was a man crawling up the mountain with us.

So ask yourself—do you want the monument?

Or the man?

Do you want the Hallmark version that looks great on a coffee mug?

Or the firestarter who told you that your greatest enemy is the comfort you refuse to abandon?

Because what they left out is exactly what makes his story dangerous enough to work.

28

Influence on Tony Robbins, Bob Proctor, and More

Napoleon Hill didn't just write Think and Grow Rich. He laid the foundation for an entire industry. Every motivational speaker, manifestation coach, personal development guru, and corporate mindset trainer you've ever heard of owes a debt—direct or stolen—to the man who first dared to say, "Your thoughts are the source of your results."

He built the stage.

Everyone else just came up after him and tweaked the lighting.

Let's be clear: Hill didn't create positive thinking. He didn't invent ambition. But he systematized it. He gave it shape. Structure. He turned scattered truths into a battle plan. And once that structure existed, the next generation picked it up and started cashing in.

Some acknowledged him. Some didn't.

But they all built their empires on his bones.

Tony Robbins: Hill with Firepower

Tony Robbins is the modern giant of personal development. Massive seminars, high-performance coaching, interventions, peak state physiology. He's Hill 2.0—louder, faster, and branded to the teeth.

But strip it all back, and Robbins' philosophy is pure Hill:

Clarity of purpose → Hill's Definiteness of Purpose

State management and belief shaping → Hill's Autosuggestion and Faith

Massive action → Hill's Persistence and Decision

Modeling successful people → Hill's Master Mind principle

Robbins built a billion-dollar brand using the framework Hill mapped out in 1937. He just added strobe lights and stadiums. What Robbins really sells is emotional access to Hill's ideas. He takes them off the page and forces you to feel them.

Robbins even said it: "I read Think and Grow Rich at 17. It changed my life."

Of course it did. It gave him the manual.

Bob Proctor: The Disciple

If Tony was the showman, Bob Proctor was the monk.

Proctor lived and breathed Hill. He didn't just teach the principles—he preached them. For over fifty years, he built an entire life around Think and Grow Rich, giving seminars, coaching programs, and corporate trainings centered almost exclusively around Hill's core philosophy.

His signature line? "If you can see it in your mind, you can hold it in your hand."

That's pure Napoleon Hill.

Proctor turned Hill's ideas into a religion—complete with rituals, repetition, and absolute faith in the power of thought to shape reality. He even credited Hill with pulling him out of poverty and giving him the mindset to build wealth.

The difference?

Hill figured it out while fighting for survival. Proctor systematized it in peacetime.

Still, the respect was real. Bob Proctor might as well have been the Pope of Hill's empire.

Rhonda Byrne: The Secret Weapon

Rhonda Byrne's The Secret hit like a thunderclap in 2006. Oprah's endorsement. The Law of Attraction on every TV screen. Vision boards, vibrations, the universe conspiring to give you everything you want.

But none of it was new.

It was Hill—wrapped in pop spirituality and sprinkled with cosmic glitter.

Byrne built The Secret on Hill's most mystical threads: the power of thought, the broadcasting brain, the ether, the subconscious mind, the sixth sense. Hill said all of it first. But he said it before Instagram existed—before it could be commodified into cute mantras and montages of people thinking about Ferraris until they showed up in the driveway.

Byrne made it marketable.

Hill made it dangerous.

What The Secret lacked in depth, it made up for in reach. But behind every manifestation coach and Law of Attraction influencer selling "abundance frequencies" and "aligned money mindset" is Napoleon Hill whispering through the centuries.

He was the source. The current. The signal.

They just turned up the volume.

The Echo Chamber Hill Built

You can see Hill's fingerprints on every corner of modern self-help:

"Thoughts become things" → Hill's Thought is the beginning of all riches

"You are the average of the five people you spend the most time with" → Hill's Master Mind alliance

"What you focus on expands" → Hill's Autosuggestion and the Subconscious Mind

"The universe is responding to your vibration" → Hill's Ether and Infinite Intelligence

"Money is a frequency" → Hill's Spiritualized thought attracts physical wealth

None of these lines are original anymore. Because Hill made them inevitable. He set the rules, and the world's been remixing them ever since.

Even Silicon Valley, the startup scene, hustle culture—they're all infected with Hill's core virus: That success begins with belief, and belief begins with choice.

From Philosopher to Formula

And here's the irony: most of these modern gurus made far more money from Hill's work than Hill ever did himself.

They got to ride the cleaned-up wave. They sold Hill's system without the scandal, the bankruptcy, the years of drifting, the existential war. They branded it, scaled it, licensed it, coached it, TED Talked it, and scaled it to the moon.

Hill lived it. Survived it.

They just monetized it.

But in a way, that was Hill's plan all along.

He wasn't trying to be the face of success forever. He was trying to plant seeds that outlived him.

And he did.

Whether his name is front and center or buried in the footnotes, Hill is everywhere. His ideas flow through Robbins, Proctor, Byrne, Vishen Lakhiani, Grant Cardone, and every manifestation page with 100k followers.

He built the engine.

They just repainted the hood.

29

How the Law of Attraction
Repackaged Hill's Ideas

The Law of Attraction didn't start in 2006 with The Secret. It didn't start with Rhonda Byrne. It didn't start with New Age Instagram influencers selling crystal-charged journals and $1,111 "abundance workshops." All that noise? It's just Hill with a filter.

Because Think and Grow Rich was the original blueprint for the Law of Attraction—before it had a name, before it got watered down, before it was turned into spiritual candy for people who wanted results without responsibility.

Rhonda didn't invent it. She remixed it.

What Hill laid out was raw, hardwired mental power: belief backed by action, directed by purpose, fueled by obsession, and reinforced by constant repetition. What the Law of Attraction crowd did was slap glitter on it and call it "alignment."

Same skeleton. Different outfit.

From Burning Desire to "Just Ask the Universe"
Hill starts with Desire. Not preference. Not vague hope. Burning, borderline-irrational, obsession-level desire.

He said you had to want it like your life depends on it. You had to write it down. Visualize it. Speak it. Repeat it. Obsess until it became part of your identity.

Now fast-forward to modern Law of Attraction content: "If you want something, just ask the universe. Think positively. Feel good. Let it flow to you."

Feel the difference?

Hill taught command. The LOA teaches wishful alignment.

Hill said desire was the engine. The Law of Attraction crowd treats it like a birthday candle. One is about willing something into existence. The other is about hoping it lands in your lap.

Autosuggestion vs. Affirmation Theater

Hill's autosuggestion wasn't cute. It was militant. He told you to program your subconscious with deliberate, emotionally-charged statements of intent—twice a day, minimum. Repetition, feeling, clarity. No fluff.

His formula wasn't "say nice things in the mirror." It was: brainwash yourself until your subconscious can no longer accept failure as an option.

Today? Autosuggestion has been reduced to affirmations on pastel backgrounds:

"I am wealthy."

"I am enough."

"I am the vibration of abundance."

Maybe. But that's not what Hill meant. He didn't want you to affirm. He wanted you to reprogram your psychological operating system. The Law of Attraction took that engine and turned it into a screensaver.

Infinite Intelligence Becomes "The Universe"

Hill wasn't shy about his mysticism. He spoke of Infinite Intelligence, the unseen realm of knowledge and inspiration that you could tune into once your mind was in the right frequency.

Sound familiar?

That's what the Law of Attraction calls the Universe. It's the same concept—just repackaged for a broader, softer audience. Hill believed that when your thoughts were saturated with belief and backed by action, they connected to something bigger than you. A field of potential. A cosmic mainframe. And from there, synchronicity began.

But Hill wasn't passive about it. He didn't say, "Let the Universe decide." He said: Command reality like it's a subordinate. But only once you've earned the right to.

That part—the personal responsibility piece—got stripped out in the translation.

The result? A philosophy that still works for the few willing to live it like Hill meant it—but one that leaves most people frustrated, because they were sold a fantasy instead of a fight.

"Vibrate Higher" vs. Organize and Execute

One of Hill's most underrated principles is Organized Planning—the exact part the Law of Attraction crowd tries to skip.

Hill knew that thought was the seed—but execution was the harvest. Visualizing isn't enough. Feeling good isn't enough. If you don't turn your goals into a plan of attack, and that plan into daily action, then all the "vibrations" in the world won't save you.

The LOA world made the dangerous mistake of treating manifestation as passive magnetism—like good vibes were currency. But Hill warned: If you don't back belief with motion, you're a drifter.

That's the part that gets lost when you turn a war manual into a mood board.

The Core Message: Belief as Power

At their core, both Think and Grow Rich and the Law of Attraction teach one thing:

Belief shapes reality.

But only Hill made it clear that belief alone is not enough. Belief must be enforced. Backed by decision. Shielded by discipline. Hardened through persistence. It must become a state of being, not just a good mood or a hopeful mantra.

The Law of Attraction, as it's now sold, is Hill with the brakes on.

Hill was offensive. Demanding. His system asks you to kill your excuses, take full responsibility, and go to war with your own programming. The Law of Attraction skips that and goes straight to "trust the universe."

That's why most people read The Secret, smile, and stay broke.

And why people who read Think and Grow Rich, apply it, and endure the friction—win.

So yes, the Law of Attraction repackaged Hill's ideas.

But they didn't improve them.

They diluted them.

They made them safer, more palatable, more profitable.

But Hill wasn't here to make you feel good.

He was here to wake you the hell up.

30

From Hustle Culture to Spiritual Capitalism

What started with Think and Grow Rich has mutated into something Hill himself might not even recognize. His work, once a firestarter for personal agency and self-mastery, has been hijacked, chopped up, repackaged, and sold back to the public as a bizarre hybrid: spiritual capitalism—where hustle culture meets cosmic law, and where your bank account supposedly mirrors your vibrational alignment.

It's no longer enough to work hard. Now you have to align energetically with your goals. You're not just closing deals—you're "manifesting abundance." And if it doesn't work? Must be your frequency. Not your plan. Not your execution. Your frequency.

This is the Frankenstein Hill helped build—without meaning to.

Hustle Culture: Hill's Blueprint with the Brakes Cut

Let's start with hustle culture.

It's Hill's DNA, no question. From definiteness of purpose to organized planning, persistence, decision, and faith, the core of Think and Grow Rich is about relentless forward motion. Action over excuses. Thought backed by discipline. Hustle culture took that and removed the nuance.

Instead of inner alignment and strategic vision, we got:

Grind 24/7

Sleep when you're dead

If you're not making six figures by 25, you're a loser

Millionaire morning routines or bust

Hill would've seen this and raised an eyebrow. Because while he preached obsession, he also emphasized clarity. The grind was never the point. Purpose was. And when hustle becomes a substitute for vision, you're not thinking and growing rich—you're just bleeding energy for the sake of being seen grinding.

But hustle culture sold. It turned Hill's principles into dopamine hits. And it gave the insecure a way to feel successful just by looking busy.

That's not personal growth. That's ego with a productivity planner.

Then Came the Flip: Hustle Goes Woo-Woo

But hustle couldn't last on its own. Burnout is real. So what did the market do?

It evolved.

Enter spiritual capitalism—where wealth isn't earned, it's channeled. Where "doing the inner work" is a strategy, and where your income becomes a reflection of your spiritual worthiness.

This is where Hill's ideas got tossed into the blender with yoga poses, moon cycles, and talk of "divine feminine business models."

Now, instead of action plans, you're told to "lean back and receive." Instead of working, you're "collapsing time." Instead of failing and adjusting, you're "clearing limiting beliefs."

It's no longer about building something real—it's about "calling it in."

Manifesting. Intending. Vibrating.

And charging $4,444 for a Zoom course on how to do it.

Hill Taught Personal Power—Not Magical Thinking

Let's be clear: Hill believed in the metaphysical. He talked about the ether, Infinite Intelligence, the subconscious, even a sixth sense. But he never taught magical thinking. He didn't say "Just believe and receive." He said, burn the boats and take the beach.

His process was brutal:

Know what you want.

Obsess over it.

Feed it to your subconscious.

Build a plan.

Execute it relentlessly.

Fail, adapt, and persist until it's real.

That's not spiritual bypassing.

That's spiritual warfare.

But spiritual capitalism took that sacred tension between thought and action and turned it into a shopping cart. It said, "You don't need to execute. You just need to align." And people bought it, because alignment sounds better than risk. It sounds cleaner than grinding. And it feels more enlightened than selling with urgency.

The Sacred Became Marketable

This is where Hill's legacy enters dangerous territory.

Because now we live in a world where:

"Money is energy" gets used to justify predatory pricing.

"Your outer world reflects your inner world" becomes an excuse to blame people for their poverty.

"Charge your worth" becomes a justification for turning spirituality into a high-ticket coaching funnel.

None of this is what Hill meant.

Hill wanted people to wake up. To take back their minds. To use belief as a tool, not a crutch. To become creators, not consumers of empowerment. But spiritual capitalism turned that call to action into a luxury brand. A lifestyle. A perfectly curated Instagram aesthetic.

It turned personal growth into performance.

And that's not growth at all.

The Real Revolution Hill Was Trying to Start

If Hill were alive to see what's been done with his work, he'd probably be impressed by the scale—and disgusted by the substance.

Because he wasn't trying to create coaches who sell manifestation. He was trying to liberate minds from drift. He was trying to build a new kind of human—self-governing, visionary, disciplined, and free.

He didn't want your vibe.

He wanted your victory.

He didn't care about your aura.

He cared about your results.

Hill's philosophy wasn't about looking successful or "feeling into" wealth. It was about becoming the kind of person who demands it, earns it, and multiplies it.

And the irony?

The more commercialized and spiritualized his legacy becomes, the more drift he would've seen infecting the movement built in his name.

So if you want to really honor Hill?

Don't just hustle.

Don't just vibrate.

Master your mind, direct your energy, and dominate your life.

Everything else is branding.

31

Was Hill a Fraud, a Visionary, or Both?

It's the question that haunts every great contradiction: Was he a fraud? Or a visionary? With Napoleon Hill, the answer is uncomfortable.

It's both.

And that's not a cop-out—it's the only honest answer. Because to understand Hill is to accept that brilliance often walks hand-in-hand with delusion, and that sometimes the man selling you the map is still lost in the woods himself.

Hill was a flawed messenger. But the message still hit like a revelation.

The Case for Fraud

Let's lay it out.

There's no evidence Andrew Carnegie ever gave Hill a secret 20-year assignment.

No proof he interviewed 500 of the most powerful men of the era.

No documentation. No letters. No corroborating witness statements. Nothing.

For a man who built his empire on the idea of credibility through access, the receipts just aren't there. It's not just that they're missing—it's that every time someone goes looking, the paper trail evaporates. Like a ghost story.

Then there's the pattern of failed businesses, unpaid debts, lawsuits, broken partnerships. Hill didn't stumble once or twice. He made a career out of promising more than he could deliver, then skipping town, reinventing himself, and starting over under a new name with the same old playbook.

In court filings, he was accused of fraud, misrepresentation, and deceptive business practices. Not once. Repeatedly.

To say none of that matters is naïve.

But to say it cancels everything?

That's just as wrong.

The Case for Visionary

Because now ask yourself:

Why, if Hill was a complete fraud, do his ideas work?

Why do countless millionaires, CEOs, creators, athletes, and everyday people swear by Think and Grow Rich?

Why has it sold over 100 million copies?

Why is it still being read today—not as a historical curiosity, but as a living philosophy?

Because Hill tapped into something deeper than data. He took universal truths—some ancient, some emerging—and gave them form. He wasn't a scientist. He was a system-builder. He was the first to distill the nebulous forces of belief, desire, persistence, and visualization into a weaponized framework for personal transformation.

He didn't invent success.

He decoded it.

And he handed it to the world in thirteen principles that, when applied, still produce results. No crystals. No shortcuts. Just hard mental work and unrelenting internal discipline.

Visionary? Absolutely.

Hill saw the power of the subconscious mind before neuroscience caught up. He talked about vibrational energy, neural programming, and quantum-like thought transmission before those words meant anything to the mainstream.

He may have lied about Carnegie.

But he told the truth about you.

The Tension Between Myth and Message

The real problem is that most people can't hold two truths at once.

They want to believe Hill was either a flawless prophet or a snake oil salesman. Black or white. But the truth lives in the gray:

He did inflate his credentials.

He did build success on shaky ethical ground.

He did deliver wisdom that continues to change lives.

That's not contradiction.

That's human nature under pressure.

Hill was preaching success while struggling to survive. He was teaching others how to master their minds while fighting like hell to control his own. His failures didn't disprove his philosophy—they proved its necessity.

He wasn't a polished success story. He was the test subject.

And what emerged from that lab of chaos was a system that has helped more people than most "legitimate" educators or life coaches could dream of.

The Real Fraud Is In the Sanitization

If there's any fraud to be worried about now, it's not Hill—it's the way his legacy has been scrubbed clean. The real fraud is the branding. The corporate polish. The Instagram quotes without context. The leadership seminars that quote Hill without mentioning Outwitting the Devil or the mental breakdowns or the repeated bankruptcies.

Hill was real.

It's the retelling of Hill that's fake.

Because what makes Hill valuable isn't that he was perfect—it's that he wasn't. That he fell flat, failed publicly, got sued, got up, started again, and still believed.

He lived the war he wrote about.

And whether you want to call that delusion or vision, it doesn't change the fact that what he left behind works.

If you do.

So Was He a Fraud? Yes. A Visionary? Also Yes.

He sold dreams he sometimes couldn't deliver.

He exaggerated his story to make the truth more palatable.

He shaped the self-help industry while often failing to help himself.

But he never stopped fighting for the belief that human beings could rise above circumstance, conditioning, and fear.

That's not fraud.

That's faith on fire.

Hill didn't always live up to his principles.

But he had the guts to write them down anyway.

And that takes more courage than most "legitimate" thinkers will ever know.

32

The Ethics of Belief-Based Success

At the heart of Napoleon Hill's philosophy is one explosive idea: You can think your way into wealth, power, and freedom. Not through luck. Not through lineage. Through belief. But belief isn't neutral. It's not just an internal compass. It's a tool—a dangerous one—and like all powerful tools, it can be used to build or to burn.

So here's the uncomfortable question:

Is it ethical to tell people that belief creates success?

Hill thought so. Millions of readers agree. But belief-based success also opens the door to delusion, victim-blaming, spiritual bypassing, and a toxic inversion of responsibility where everything is your fault—even the things you couldn't control.

This isn't just a philosophical issue.

It's moral territory.

And most of the people cashing checks off belief never stop to question the cost.

The Weaponization of "Thoughts Become Things"

Hill's idea—that thoughts are causative, that belief is creative—was revolutionary. It shattered the old paradigms of class, destiny, and inherited power. It said the poor man could rise. The outcast could conquer. The dreamer could build an empire from thin air.

It was beautiful.

And when applied with discipline and honesty, it works.

But here's where things get dark: when belief is sold without context, without ethics, and without the acknowledgment of external realities—it becomes a whip.

"You're poor because you didn't think hard enough."

"You're sick because your mindset was weak."

"You lost everything because you weren't aligned."

This is the shadow side of belief-based success. The side that punishes failure as a moral flaw. The side that shames struggle instead of examining systems. The side that tells you you're the architect of your reality—even when someone else burned your house down.

Hill never said belief replaces effort. But modern self-help did. And that distortion is ethically criminal.

The Danger of Selling Certainty

Belief is powerful. But it's not perfect.

Hill's greatest misstep wasn't in teaching people to believe—it was in teaching them to believe without showing them how to deal with failure when belief isn't enough.

Because sometimes, belief doesn't work the way you want it to.

You get sick.

You get cheated.

You lose the business.

You lose the child.

And if you've been told your belief was the only variable that mattered, then what happens next is spiritual collapse. Shame. Guilt. Self-loathing.

That's not empowerment.

That's indoctrination.

The ethical problem with belief-based success is that it doesn't always leave space for nuance, trauma, timing, or reality. It's too often sold as guaranteed. As if the universe is a vending machine that dispenses success to those who vibrate hard enough.

Hill was more careful than that. He warned of drift. He warned of fear. He warned that most people wouldn't apply his principles because they'd give up too soon.

But today? Those warnings are gone.

And what's left is a moral vacuum.

Responsibility vs. Blame

Hill was obsessed with personal responsibility. He didn't believe in luck. He believed in cause and effect. In thinking, planning, and persistence. He wasn't wrong.

But there's a razor's edge between responsibility and blame.

Telling someone, "You're responsible for your success," is empowering.

Telling someone, "You're to blame for your pain," is cruel.

Belief becomes unethical when it's used to shame instead of strengthen. When it's used to sell fantasies instead of teach discipline. When it's used to deflect hard questions about systems, trauma, inequality, or chance.

Hill's ethics were rooted in sovereignty—your mind is yours to shape. But sovereignty doesn't mean isolation. And belief doesn't mean control over every variable in the universe.

That's where most modern self-help fails.

It doesn't teach people how to hold both truth and tragedy. How to say, "I believe fully—and still, I might fail." Or, "I did everything right, and the world hit back anyway."

Ethical belief acknowledges that you're not God.

You're just finally acting like you're not a victim.

So, What's Ethical Belief Look Like?

Here's what Hill got right—and what modern successors need to remember:

Belief should be paired with strategy.

Vision with planning. Imagination with execution. Otherwise, it's fantasy dressed as work.

Belief should be taught with humility.

Not everyone starts at the same line. Some are climbing mountains while others are running on flat ground. Pretending mindset is the only variable is intellectually dishonest.

Belief should be tested.

If your philosophy can't survive failure, it's not belief. It's dogma. Real belief holds even when the scoreboard says you're losing.

Belief should liberate, not accuse.

If you're using someone's belief system to judge their outcomes, you're not a coach—you're a tyrant.

Hill's Legacy: Empowerment, Not Absolutism

So was Hill unethical?

No.

But those who ripped his ideas from context, slapped them on Instagram, and sold $5,000 manifestation courses might be.

Hill wanted people to wake up. To claim ownership of their minds. To act. That's empowerment. That's ethical. But he also admitted—he drifted too. He failed. He feared. He lost battles with his own subconscious.

That's what makes him trustworthy.

Because belief isn't perfect.

But it's the only place you can start.

The ethics of belief-based success come down to this:

Teach people to believe, yes. But also teach them to fight, to fall, and to rise again without shame.

That's what Hill was trying to do.

And if we're going to carry his legacy forward—

We'd better get it right.

33

The Dangers of Blind Faith in Self-Help Gurus

In the world Napoleon Hill helped build—this vast industry of self-help, success, and personal development—there's one thing more dangerous than failure:

Blind faith.

Because once you hand over your discernment, once you replace your judgment with someone else's charisma, you're no longer on a journey of empowerment. You're in a cult with nicer lighting. And the modern self-help movement is flooded with charismatic salesmen who talk like prophets, sell like predators, and promise salvation for the price of a coaching package.

Hill wasn't the first. But he was the prototype.

And if you don't question the message—or the messenger—you're not chasing success.

You're drifting into delusion.

When Belief Becomes Submission

Hill told you to believe in yourself. To feed your subconscious like a machine. To repeat affirmations until your internal operating system couldn't accept failure. Powerful stuff—when aimed inward.

But self-help culture twisted the formula.

Now you're told to believe in the guru. To surrender your logic. To silence your doubts. To see any criticism as "low vibration," and any challenge as "ego resistance."

That's not belief.

That's indoctrination.

The moment belief becomes submission, you've lost the plot. You're no longer thinking and growing rich. You're outsourcing your mind to a man with a microphone.

That's not empowerment. That's enslavement with a smile.

The Cult of Personality

Self-help used to be about systems. Principles. Philosophies.

Now? It's about personalities.

It's about the influencer. The voice. The "brand." Gurus have replaced teachers. And once the teacher becomes the product, the truth dies in the marketing.

They sell identity, not insight.

They preach transparency, while hiding broken marriages, failed businesses, and therapy-worthy egos behind a wall of staged photos and curated testimonials.

They create dependency—not independence.

And here's the trick: the better they are at pretending to be you, the easier it is for you to stop thinking. Because they don't look like manipulators. They look like reflections of who you want to be.

Until you realize you've been copying a mask.

The Gaslighting Loop

Here's how it works:

The guru tells you success is guaranteed if you follow the system.

You follow the system.

It doesn't work the way they promised.

You question it—and they say you're the problem.

"You didn't want it badly enough."

"You weren't aligned."

"You still have limiting beliefs."

It's not just manipulation—it's spiritual gaslighting. You start doubting yourself instead of the person who just took your money. You internalize the failure as evidence of your own brokenness. And that keeps you coming back—for more coaching, more programs, more answers that never arrive.

This isn't self-help.

It's self-harm disguised as growth.

The Broken Mirror of Hill's Legacy

Now here's where it gets complicated—Napoleon Hill had followers too. He had people who bought into him as much as they bought into his message. And some of those people walked away burned. Scammed. Abandoned.

Because even Hill—visionary that he was—sometimes became the guru he warned against.

He didn't always deliver. He promised things he couldn't back up. He left failed ventures in his wake and refused to take full accountability. That doesn't make him evil. It makes him human. But it also makes him a case study in what happens when belief in the message turns into blind faith in the man.

Hill's teachings survive because they work.

But Hill's life? It proves that no guru, no matter how enlightened, is above scrutiny.

And if Hill himself couldn't live up to the system all the time, what makes us think today's Instagram prophet with the six-figure funnel has it all figured out?

Real Growth Demands Discernment

The self-help world thrives on certainty. Clear steps. Motivational slogans. "Just believe." "Trust the process." "You are the only thing standing in your way."

But real growth?

It's messy. Uncomfortable. Complex. It requires self-doubt. Inquiry. Pushback. Sometimes, the greatest act of personal power is not saying "Yes, coach"—but saying "Prove it."

Discernment is not negativity.

Skepticism is not resistance.

Saying "no" to a guru doesn't mean you're scared of success—it means you're awake.

Hill's real message wasn't "follow me." It was "master yourself."

And if someone is teaching you otherwise—if they're demanding obedience, selling salvation, and punishing questions—run.

You don't need a guru.

You need your own authority.

The danger of blind faith isn't just that it leads you astray.

It's that it convinces you the leash around your neck is a ladder to freedom.

34

Timeless Wisdom in a World Addicted to Mediocrity

Napoleon Hill's words weren't designed for a soft culture. He didn't write Think and Grow Rich for the perpetually offended, the spiritually lazy, or the screen-scrolling dopamine junkies of the 21st century. He wrote it for the few—the misfits, the builders, the ones tired of watching the world rot under the weight of comfort and compliance.

And that's why his wisdom still matters.

Because the world has changed, but the disease hasn't: mediocrity. It's just been rebranded. Made palatable. Celebrated, even. We hand out trophies for it. We base entire economies around it. We feed people a diet of distraction and entitlement, and when they choke, we tell them they just need better "work-life balance."

Hill didn't play that game.

He offered a brutal antidote to mediocrity: personal power, radical responsibility, and uncompromising vision.

And in today's culture?

That's practically heresy.

The Culture of Convenience

Modern society has made mediocrity look respectable.

You're not lazy, you're "protecting your peace."

You're not avoiding discomfort, you're "setting boundaries."

You're not stuck in a rut, you're "taking time to recalibrate."

Hill would call it out for what it is: drift.

His entire philosophy was built on resisting the gravitational pull of mediocrity—the unconscious, half-dead state where you think you're living because you're busy, but you're really just coasting. And today, drift is everywhere.

You see it in people who confuse motion for progress. Who post about their dreams but never touch the damn blueprint. Who talk about alignment, but can't commit to anything longer than a weekend challenge.

Hill said definiteness of purpose was the first law of achievement.

Today, purpose is optional—as long as the brand looks good and the algorithm agrees.

Wisdom Doesn't Expire—People Just Get Softer

Every generation thinks it's smarter than the last. But intelligence without will is just decoration. And that's where we are now: a society that knows everything and does nothing.

We have access to more knowledge than Hill ever dreamed of. But what do most people do with it?

Scroll. Compare. Freeze. Complain.

Napoleon Hill didn't have ChatGPT. He didn't have YouTube tutorials or online masterminds or Reddit threads full of productivity hacks. What he had was urgency. And fire. And hunger. And that's what gave his wisdom weight.

He didn't care how much you knew.

He cared what you did.

That message is timeless because human nature doesn't change. We still seek comfort over challenge. We still fear criticism more than failure. We still wait for permission instead of declaring purpose.

And Hill's voice still punches through all of it like a war drum:

"Whatever the mind can conceive and believe, it can achieve."

But only if you move.

The War Against Average Is Internal

Hill's real genius wasn't just in showing you how to win. It was in showing you who the real enemy was: you. Your fear. Your excuses. Your drift.

He didn't point to society, or the economy, or your childhood trauma. He pointed to the mirror.

In today's world, that's offensive.

We're trained to look outward for blame and inward for comfort. To view victimhood as identity and mediocrity as virtue. But Hill's timeless truth still slices through the fog:

"You are the master of your fate. The captain of your soul."

Not your coach. Not your therapist. Not your parents. You.

That truth hurts. That's why most people will reject it.

Because once you accept it, you can't hide anymore.

You can't stay mediocre and blame the world.

You either rise—or admit that you never planned to.

Why Hill Still Matters

Hill's work doesn't trend on TikTok. It doesn't feed the algorithm. It's not cute. It demands more than attention—it demands transformation. And that's exactly why it still matters.

Because while the world gets softer, his principles get sharper.

While people seek hacks, Hill offers discipline.

While most chase validation, Hill demands vision.

And in a culture where everyone wants to "feel good," Hill dares to ask: What are you building? What are you becoming? What will be left behind when the lights go out and the applause dies?

That's why Think and Grow Rich is still here.

Because truth doesn't care about trends.

Wisdom doesn't rot.

And personal power doesn't expire.

So yes, the world is addicted to mediocrity.

But Hill gave you the cure.

You just have to have the guts to swallow it.

35

The Value of Personal Responsibility and Belief

I f there's one thread that runs through everything Napoleon Hill ever wrote—through the polished pages of Think and Grow Rich, through the chaos of his life, through the buried fire of Outwitting the Devil—it's this:

You are responsible. And what you believe matters.

Not in a slogan. Not in a hashtag. Not in a "morning affirmation" kind of way.

In a foundational way.

In a your life depends on it kind of way.

And that truth—uncomfortable, offensive, liberating—is the final gift Hill gave the world. Not a guarantee. Not a shortcut. But a sword.

Because personal responsibility and belief, when actually lived, are the death of helplessness. And in a society addicted to victimhood, they are revolutionary weapons.

Responsibility Is the Gateway Drug to Freedom

Hill never said it would be easy. He never said it would be fair. What he said was this:

"You are where you are because of the thoughts you've allowed to dominate your mind."

To the untrained ear, that sounds cruel. Like blame. Like ignoring hardship, systems, trauma. But Hill wasn't denying the existence of suffering—he was attacking the paralysis that suffering breeds.

Responsibility isn't about guilt.

It's about authority.

It means you're not waiting anymore. Not blaming. Not hoping some guru or government or algorithm is going to save you. It means you've picked up the damn pen and started writing your own script.

And belief? That's the ink.

Belief Isn't Comfort—It's Ammunition

Hill understood something most of today's soft philosophers don't: belief is not about feeling good.

Belief is directional. It tells your brain what to look for. It filters your reality. It shapes what you're willing to tolerate, pursue, or reject. Hill didn't care about positive thinking for the sake of mental fluff. He weaponized it.

Belief, in his world, is a command to the subconscious.

You tell your mind what's true. Then you back it up with focus, repetition, and relentless execution—until reality folds under the weight of your internal certainty.

But here's the hard truth:

You don't get belief by reading another quote.

You get belief by choosing it—and then proving it through action, daily, until your life finally gets the memo.

Responsibility + Belief = Sovereignty

This is what Hill was really after—not just success, but sovereignty.

The ability to govern yourself. To be unswayed by drift. To live on your own terms, build by your own rules, and rise or fall based on your own will.

That's rare now.

We live in a world of outsourcing: outsource your goals to your job, your emotions to your therapist, your future to the state, your self-worth to a screen. Hill said take it back. All of it.

The responsibility is yours.

The belief is yours.

And so the outcome—good or bad—is also yours.

That's terrifying.

But it's also the only thing that will ever set you free.

Why It Still Matters

Hill's ideas survive because they can't be killed. You can bury them under mediocrity, you can wrap them in marketing, you can sell them through watered-down gurus—but the core remains:

You have the power to shape your reality.

You are not a victim of circumstance, unless you choose to be.

Thought is cause. Action is reinforcement. Reality is the result.

People call that naïve now. They call it outdated. But you know what's outdated?

Waiting.

Blaming.

Excusing.

Drifting.

Personal responsibility and belief are timeless because they don't need to be trendy. They just need to be true. And once you accept that truth, you start walking a path most people will never touch:

A path where nothing is promised.

But everything is possible.

Hill's Final Lesson

Hill didn't live a perfect life.

But he lived a transparent war with the human condition—and he shared the strategy with anyone willing to pick up the sword.

The system works.

Not because it's magical.

But because it requires you to become something greater than who you were yesterday.

And the first step is the hardest:

Take responsibility.

Choose belief.

Then get to work.

That's it.

That's the gospel Hill died trying to preach.
And if you've made it this far, you already know—
That kind of gospel isn't for the world.
It's for the few.

36

The Seductive Power of Self-Created Mythology

Napoleon Hill didn't just write about success—he performed it. He didn't just sell a book—he sold a story. A myth. And that myth—crafted, curated, exaggerated, and repeated—wasn't just part of the package.

It was the package.

Because here's the raw, uncomfortable truth no one wants to say out loud:

Sometimes, the myth is more powerful than the man.

Hill understood that before any of the modern-day brand-builders, influencers, or self-help saints ever figured it out. He knew that people don't follow logic—they follow narrative. They don't crave data. They crave destiny. And when the truth is too slow, too boring, or too ugly, the myth steps in.

And we believe it—because we need to.

A Story Stronger Than Fact

The Carnegie story is the crown jewel of Hill's mythology. A secret assignment. A 20-year quest. Hundreds of interviews with titans of industry. A blueprint of wealth delivered by divine capitalist revelation.

It's beautiful.

It's also completely unverifiable.

No documents. No letters. No records. Just Hill's word. And you know what? Most people never question it. Because the power of the story overrides the need for proof.

That's the seductive trick of self-created mythology. It bypasses the logical brain. It speaks to the soul. It whispers, If he was chosen, maybe I'm chosen too. And in that moment, you're not buying a book—you're buying into possibility.

That's what Hill was really selling.

Not steps.

Not principles.

Permission.

We Don't Just Tolerate Myth—We Crave It

Our culture pretends to love authenticity, but that's a lie. What we love is performance dressed as truth. We worship confidence. We crave the origin story. The turning point. The "zero to hero" arc. And when someone presents it with enough conviction, we don't just believe it—we repeat it.

Hill gave the world exactly what it wanted:

A poor boy from the backwoods of Virginia

A divine encounter with one of the richest men in history

A mission to decode success

A system so powerful it could resurrect your life from the ashes

It's the American Dream with a metaphysical upgrade.

And the more his real life unraveled—financial collapse, lawsuits, failure—the more the myth had to hold the line. Because when reality disappoints, the myth becomes necessary.

That's what makes it so seductive.

The myth doesn't flinch.

The myth doesn't fail.

The myth lives forever.

The Risk: Believing the Myth More Than the Message

Here's the danger—and it's not just about Hill.

When you fall in love with the myth more than the message, you stop asking questions. You stop thinking. You drift into hero-worship. And that's when you become easy to manipulate.

Because now it's not about whether the ideas work. It's about who said them. And suddenly, the authority of the messenger replaces the effectiveness of the method.

You see it everywhere in the self-help world:

People quoting their coach like scripture.

Blind loyalty to personal brands.

"If it worked for him, it must work for me"—even when it doesn't.

Hill never asked you to worship him. But the myth made it easy to do so.

Because worship is easier than work.

Believing in the legend is easier than becoming one.

Mythology Is a Tool—If You Control It

Now here's where the power flips.

Mythology isn't evil. In fact, it's essential. Every great movement, every revolution, every personal transformation begins with narrative. With identity. With belief in something bigger than your current self.

Hill wasn't wrong to craft a myth.

He just never fully owned it.

He let the story outrun the man.

But you? You can use mythology like a weapon—if you stay conscious of the difference between story and reality. Use it to shape your identity. To set the tone. To create urgency and meaning in your life.

Build your own mythology.

Craft your own arc.

Not to lie—but to live louder than your fear.

That's what Hill did. For better or worse.

And it's what every leader, creator, and legend continues to do today.

The Final Seduction

The myth is never about the man.

It's about you.

Hill's story endures not because it was all true—but because it felt possible. He showed us what it looks like to believe so deeply in an outcome that you start bending reality to match it. Whether or not it all happened exactly as he said?

It doesn't matter.

Because in the end, the seduction of self-created mythology is this:

If you speak the future boldly enough, people stop caring about your past.

And if you live the myth long enough—

Sometimes it becomes real.

37

Separating the Man from the Message

Napoleon Hill was not the man he claimed to be.

And that's okay.

Because the power of his work was never dependent on his perfection—it was dependent on your willingness to apply it. The man failed. The message didn't. And the sooner we stop confusing the two, the sooner we can use what's true and discard what's noise.

We live in a culture obsessed with tearing down statues. If the messenger stumbles, we burn the message. If the author sins, we ban the book. It's lazy, cowardly moralism dressed as integrity. And it's killing off wisdom faster than ignorance ever could.

So let's say it clearly:

Hill was flawed, contradictory, and unreliable at times. His principles were none of those things.

A Message Bigger Than the Messenger

Think and Grow Rich works.

That's the uncomfortable fact.

Whether Hill interviewed Carnegie or not... the system still works.

Whether he paid his debts or skipped town... the principles still produce results.

Whether he failed in business or not... his mental framework continues to build businesses.

This isn't blind loyalty—it's observation. The message survives because it transcends the man. Hill was just the delivery mechanism. A loud, obsessive, occasionally reckless transmitter for something bigger than himself.

And isn't that the point?

The greatest ideas in history rarely come from saints. They come from fire-starters. Imperfect men willing to throw their entire identity into the furnace and pull out something forged by failure, friction, and belief.

Hill was that.

So stop asking if he was worthy.

Start asking if you're ready.

Why the Fallibility Matters

If anything, Hill's mess makes the message stronger.

Because it proves the principles don't require perfection. They don't need you to be rich, polished, credentialed, or calm. They just need you to commit. Hill failed, drifted, doubted—and still built a legacy that outlived him.

That's not disqualification.

That's proof of access.

It means anyone can wield these tools. Anyone can take back control of their mind, their beliefs, their vision. You don't need to be elite. You need to be awake.

The irony?

The people who dismiss Hill because of his flaws are often the ones too scared to look at their own. It's easier to tear down a man than build your own life. But Hill never claimed to be the model. He offered the manual.

That's all he owed you.

Don't Worship. Apply.

Separating the man from the message means you don't need to defend his life to defend his work. You don't need to become a Napoleon Hill apologist. You don't even need to like him.

You just need to use the tools.

Burning desire

Faith

Autosuggestion

Specialized knowledge

Persistence

Organized planning

Mastermind alliances

Decision

They still work.

They will work—for you, or for someone else. And if you ignore them because Hill didn't live up to your standards, someone else will use them to lap you in life.

Because while you're busy moralizing the man, they're executing the message.

This is how you take the truth and make it yours.

No heroes.

No hype.

Just application.

What Hill Would Say Now

If Hill could speak now, stripped of myth and legacy, he probably wouldn't defend himself. He'd look you in the eye and say:

Yes—I failed.

Yes—I exaggerated.

Yes—I fell short more than once.

But I never stopped trying.

I never stopped writing.

I never stopped believing that man could rise—if he wanted it badly enough.

And you?

You have more tools, more freedom, more access than I ever did.

So what's your excuse?

That's the voice underneath all of Hill's work. Not a guru. Not a saint.

Just a flawed man pushing you toward your own greatness.

The Final Separation

Napoleon Hill, the man, was a contradiction.

But the message?

It's consistent, brutal, liberating.

It tells you to take control of your thoughts, demand more from your reality, and refuse to drift. It's not about motivation. It's not about feeling good.

It's about becoming someone worthy of your own vision.

So separate the man from the message. Use the truth. Burn the myth. Live the work.

Because in the end, what matters isn't who he was.

It's who you become.

38

How to Think with Hill—Not Just Grow Rich

By now, you know the game. You've seen the contradictions. You've read the truth behind the myth. Napoleon Hill wasn't a guru. He was a builder of mental weapons. He wasn't asking you to admire him—he was daring you to upgrade your operating system.

The book was never really about getting rich.

It was about how to think.

How to install a mindset that could resist drift, ignore fear, channel desire, and outwork the decay of mediocrity that infects most people's lives from birth to death.

But too many people stop at the title. They chase the riches, quote the slogans, repeat the affirmations, and skip the most important part:

Learning how to think like Napoleon Hill.

Not just what he thought.

How he thought.

That's the real inheritance.

Thinking is a Skill—Not a Trait

Hill didn't stumble into philosophy. He built it. Brick by brick. He took scattered experiences, personal failures, scraps of insight from powerful men, and years of desperation—and forged a system.

That's what thinking is: not reaction, not regurgitation, but construction.

Hill didn't wait for truth to land in his lap.

He pursued it.

He challenged his own assumptions.

He studied human behavior like a detective chasing a pattern.

He made mistakes, but he never outsourced his responsibility to anyone else. He owned his thoughts, even when they scared him.

That's the part most readers miss. They want the result—"rich"—without the internal architecture of how Hill arrived at those results.

If you want to think like Hill, you have to stop consuming and start creating meaning out of chaos.

The Hill Mindset—Deconstructed

Here's what it looks like to think with Hill in a world addicted to shortcuts:

Desire isn't a preference. It's a directive.

If you say you want something but don't restructure your life around it, Hill would say you're lying. Wanting is worthless. Burning desire creates movement.

Doubt is fuel, not failure.

Hill didn't ignore fear. He faced it, interrogated it, argued with it. He made the Devil talk. That's thinking. That's mental combat. Most people avoid that. Hill scheduled it.

Thinking is not positive. It's purposeful.

He didn't preach blind optimism. He preached control over the dominant mental narrative. That's different. That's the difference between repeating mantras and installing mental code that reroutes your identity.

Faith isn't religion. It's commitment to execution in the absence of evidence.

Hill didn't need the world to believe in his plan. He forced the world to adjust. That's faith in action. Most people wait for proof. Hill demanded results from the unseen.

The subconscious is not magic. It's mechanical.

Hill used belief the way a hacker uses a backdoor. He planted thoughts, repeated them, and watched them show up in his habits. That's not mysticism. That's neural programming—before anyone had a name for it.

That's the Hill mindset.

Not "think happy thoughts."

Think on purpose. Think like your future depends on it. Think until reality submits.

Thinking as a Weapon

Hill didn't write Think and Grow Rich for entertainment.

He wrote it as a declaration of war—on drift, fear, laziness, and societal programming. It was a manual for the mental elite. The 2% who weren't going to spend their lives blaming parents, governments, algorithms, or trauma for why they never became who they were meant to be.

If you just want to get rich, there are faster paths now. Crypto. Funnels. AI. You can make money without thinking. But you won't own yourself. And the moment the money slips, so does your identity.

But if you learn to think like Hill—you can rebuild from zero. Again and again. Because you don't just have tools.

You are the tool.

The New Rich: Mental Sovereignty

Forget the bank account.

The new definition of "rich" is this:

Clear in thought.

Ruthless in purpose.

Immune to drift.

Faithful to your vision.

Free from fear.

Unshakeable under pressure.

Mentally sovereign.

That's what Hill wanted to give you.

And it only starts with thinking.

Once you own your mind, you own your actions. Once you own your actions, you own your results. And once you own your results—you don't need anyone's permission, validation, or approval ever again.

You're not rich because you have.

You're rich because you can.

That's the Napoleon Hill that most people never meet.

Now you have.

So stop quoting him.

And start thinking with him.

39

The Reader's Role in Discerning
Truth from Hype

No matter how sharp Napoleon Hill's mind was—or how shaky his biography—one thing is absolutely true:

It's not his job to live your life.

That's your job.

And in a world drowning in hype, brand polish, spiritual marketing, and recycled soundbites, the last responsibility that still belongs to you is this:

Discernment.

Because the self-help industry isn't about truth. It's about appeal. It doesn't reward the most accurate voices—it rewards the most attractive ones. The loudest. The cleanest. The ones that make you feel empowered without making you uncomfortable.

And Hill? He was uncomfortable. Flawed. Radical. Misunderstood. Which is why his work still has teeth—if you know how to read it.

Your job now is not to worship Hill. Not to cancel him either.

Your job is to discern.

There Are No Perfect Gurus—Only Imperfect Tools

We live in a time when people treat authors like messiahs and books like doctrine. One contradiction in the author's life? The entire message gets tossed out. One flaw? Burn the legacy. One inconsistency? Invalidate the ideas.

But that's a child's game.

Adults know that tools don't need to be perfect to work.

You don't throw away a hammer because the carpenter who sold it went bankrupt. You don't abandon a map because the man who drew it had a bad sense of direction in his own life.

Hill gave you tools. Some were polished. Some were rough. Some came wrapped in myth. But if you've read this far, you know how to separate them now.

You're not here to be spoon-fed.

You're here to think for yourself.

What's True, What's Hype, and What's Yours

Hype is easy to spot—once you stop being addicted to it.

It's loud. Simple. Overpromised. It gives you a hit of motivation without asking for anything real in return. Hype says, You're already enough. Just vibe. Hype says, Buy this and the work will do itself. Hype sells you the feeling of power—without the cost of becoming powerful.

Hill didn't do that.

He gave you work. Frameworks. Inner war. He gave you 13 principles that demand effort, time, repetition, sacrifice, persistence, faith, failure, and adaptation.

That's not hype.

That's craftsmanship.

So as the reader, your job is to tell the difference.

If something feels too clean, too easy, too frictionless—it's probably hype.

If it makes you uncomfortable, demands more than you're used to, and challenges your current self-image—it's probably truth.

And the ultimate litmus test?

Does it work when your life is on fire?

Because the real value of Hill's message is that it works when everything else has stopped working.

That's what you came here for.

Not a dopamine spike.

But a damn blueprint.

The Danger of Passive Consumption

If you read Hill like a fan, you'll quote him.

If you read Hill like a student, you'll use him.

But if you read Hill like a consumer—waiting to be impressed, motivated, or entertained—then you've missed the point entirely. This book, this system, this entire philosophy is not passive. It's a mirror. A challenge. A contract.

And every page asks the same question:

What will you do now?

You can admire Hill. Dissect Hill. Quote Hill. Critique Hill. You can build a YouTube channel about his life, write articles about his fraud, or tattoo "Definiteness of Purpose" on your wrist.

None of that matters.

Only application matters.

Only transformation matters.

And no one—not Hill, not me, not any guru—can do that part for you.

The Final Discerning Act: Choose

Discerning truth from hype means reclaiming your agency.

It means saying:

*I believe what serves me—*not just what flatters me.

I think for myself—even if the crowd thinks otherwise.

I act, I test, I apply—because no one is coming to do it for me.

Hill handed you the mental blueprints for sovereignty.

He asked you to be fierce, not fragile.

To use belief as a weapon, not a pillow.

To become the kind of person whose thoughts must manifest—because your belief, your vision, and your action are so aligned that the world doesn't get a say anymore.

That's how you honor this work.

Not by believing all of it.

Not by believing none of it.

But by deciding what to build with it.

And then doing it.

40

Epilogue

By Will Stickle

Napoleon Hill was not a god. He was not a fraud. He was not a flawless master of the universe who handed down success from a gold-plated tower.

He was a man.

A brilliant, broken, driven, dangerous man who tried harder than most to crack the code of personal power—and sometimes got it right. He shaped his reality with words, some truer than others. He failed. He lied. He transformed. He survived. And from that mess, he left us a system strong enough to outlive him.

But this book—A Hill to Die On—was never about Hill alone.

It's about you.

About what you believe. What you build. What you allow. What you excuse. What you become. Hill laid down the tools. The rest is up to the reader—not to admire, not to quote, but to apply.

The time for gurus is over.

The time for sovereignty has begun.

Make your move.

www.ingramcontent.com/pod-product-compliance
Lightning Source LLC
Chambersburg PA
CBHW061807120626
46550CB00005B/2180